DANCIN' WITH HANSON

from the middle of nowhere to the top of the world

by Ravi

Pocket Books

New York   London   Toronto   Sydney   Tokyo   Singapore

Acknowledgments

My father, Ajit, for his guidance and help in publishing my story; my mother, Amrita, for pointing out my grammatical errors every day of my life; my brother Nikhil, for lending his writing talents and helping me craft my written voice; and my brother Vivek, for continuously sharing in the excitement throughout my year with the band. Thank you all for your love, enthusiasm, and support.

Lisa Clancy, Gina DiMarco, Jane Ginsberg, Patricia MacDonald, Brigid Pearson, Nancy Pines, Liz Shiflett, Donna O'Neill, Brian Blatz, Karen Clark, Lisa Feuer, Twisne Fan, Linda Dingler, and my other new friends at Pocket Books and Simon & Schuster.

Bob Capazzo, Ellen Giurleo, Jay Katz, and Steve Sabba. Thanks for handling my affairs with skill, professionalism, humor, and good nature.

Lisa Banim, Carrie Coolidge, Jeffrey Cowan, Jay Itzkowitz, Rhona Johnson, Fran Lebowitz, C.K. Lendt, and Randi Reisfeld. Thanks for all your input and advice.

Jason Browning, Mike Conti, John "Ratso" Gerardi, and Pat Harris. Thanks for your contributions.

Peter DiSalvo, Emily Frangipane, Mike Mirtsopoulos, and Duane Smith. Thanks for your opinions, contributions, enthusiasm, and unshakable friendship.

Isaac, Taylor, and Zac Hanson. Thanks for causing and sharing these amazing moments.

I dedicate this book to *opportunity*.

An Archway Paperback published by
POCKET BOOKS, a division of Simon & Schuster Inc.
1230 Avenue of the Americas, New York, NY 10020

Copyright © 1999 by Suburban Turban, Inc.

ISBN: 0-671-03598-3

First Archway Paperback printing April 1999

10 9 8 7 6 5 4 3 2 1

AN ARCHWAY PAPERBACK and colophon are registered trademarks of Simon & Schuster Inc.

Front cover photo credits: Ravi by Brian Velenchenko; Hanson © MC/Hansonopoly/Outline

Printed in the U.S.A.

Interior book design by Mark Pessoni

Table of Contents

To Lisa & Amy

Best Wishes

Introduction

Throughout 1997, I played guitar for Hanson, which was truly an amazing experience. I made many new friends and fulfilled numerous dreams. Millions of musicians work all their lives to get a "lucky break." I am one of the few who managed to secure one.

The Hanson phenomenon formed right before my eyes. Isaac, Taylor, Zac, two other backup musicians, and I rose from the "middle of nowhere" to the top of the world. To many, Hanson is a teen sensation comprising three brothers. For me, it was a group of six friends making music. It didn't begin or end that way, but that's how I felt while I was on the road with the band.

I will never forget the day it began. It was a cold winter afternoon, and I had just returned home from the school where I taught guitar. The flashing light on my answering machine begged me to press PLAY. There was only one message, a brief one from an old friend. "I passed your name along to a production coordinator at Mercury Records," he said. "They need a young guitarist for a two-week road gig—thought you might be interested." I decided to find out some more information. I called the contact instead of waiting for her to call me, and left a message on her machine. After two days and no phone call, I called again, and this time she picked up the line. She explained to me that Hanson, who were unknown at the time, had just recorded an album (using additional studio musicians) on Mercury Records and that the label was putting together a support band to help showcase the young trio at an industry convention. After two weeks, if I didn't like the band or they didn't like me, I wouldn't have to continue working with them, if that were even an option. What did I have to lose? The pay was decent, and I thought it would be fun to travel and try something different. I went for it.

The day after I accepted the job, a large envelope from Mercury Records arrived on my doorstep. Enclosed was a color copy of their first promotional photo, a press release and a demo tape. I could not believe how young they looked. Taylor, the middle brother, had a slight "bad boy" look. The older one, Isaac, had a relatively serious expression and the youngest, Zac, looked like a toddler! I couldn't help but fear that they were three obnoxious boys with egos beyond their years. But when I actually met them, I was pleasantly surprised to find that they were arguably the nicest and most sincere kids that I had ever met.

I immediately played the tape. The first cut was "Thinking of You," which I instantly liked, even though I had a hard time adapting to Taylor's youthful voice. "MMMBop" was the next song, and I thought that it was catchy. I began listening to the entire *Middle of Nowhere* album constantly. I kept a copy in my car, in my studio, and in my house. I found myself becoming a fan and was getting very excited about the project.

During my first conversation with Michael Pontecorvo, an executive from Mercury Records, I sensed that this would be an unusual experience. The first words he said to me were "Ravi, can you hold on? I have the bass player's mother on the other line." It had been a while since "moms" were part of my music scene.

My work with Hanson started as a two-week stint but turned into a year of incredible adventures. As the band evolved, I experienced the glamor and grind of one of the music industry's most visible and exploited acts. I indulged in the best of what fame had to offer, but as a sideman, I was able to walk away from the hardships that celebrities often have to endure.

Still, a band that reaches the level of success that Hanson has comes with many frustrations and headaches. Schedules were unpredictable and unreliable. We often received travel updates on an hourly basis, rarely knowing where we were going, how long we would be gone, or even if what we were discussing was actually going to happen. One of our sound engineers archived every printed schedule in a black binder, which he affectionately referred to as "the book of lies."

I was very frustrated one particular evening because I had rescheduled a recording date three times to accommodate Hanson. Since the Hanson organization did not retain the entourage and rarely paid for days off, most of us needed to maintain outside work. Our tour manager sympathized with me and summarized the situation well. "The Hansons will change their minds as they please," he said. "The rest of us, we're just dancin'."

I regularly interact with thousands of fans from around the world, often spending time with them outside the stage doors. In addition, hundreds of fans e-mail me daily, all wanting to know about my life on the road with Isaac, Taylor, and Zac. Because of the large number of questions, it is impossible for me to answer each one individually. However, I can share my Hanson stories and experiences on the following pages with everyone. With the help of my daily journal and personal camera, let me take you on the road—on the road with Hanson.

1
In the Middle of Nowhere

Mercury Records assembled the band in Hanson's hometown of Tulsa, Oklahoma. We set up shop in a very old theater that appeared as if it hadn't been used in years. The auditorium had dark walls with yellow seats, and a colorful, psychedelic banner hung from the front of the stage to the floor.

I could see mold and dust everywhere. The power supply was inconsistent and the entire structure seemed as if it might collapse at any moment. Four days into rehearsal, the local fire marshal tried to shut us down because of the questionable conditions of the building. Somehow, we managed to stay.

In some respects, this was the most interesting time in the Hanson story. No one had heard of Isaac, Taylor, and Zac—including many Tulsa locals—and no one had predicted the level of success that Hanson was about to achieve. We were a six-piece band, nothing more, nothing less. They were an average, Midwestern family, nothing more, nothing less.

Monday, March 3, 1997—
Tulsa, Rehearsal

The Hanson family arrived today returning from Los Angeles, where they had taped their first MTV video, "MMMBop."

Taylor, then thirteen, was dressed in a green sport shirt, with a single white and blue stripe, and a pair of cords. Sixteen-year-old Isaac was wearing a similar shirt in blue and a pair of black pants. Zac, eleven years old, had on a blue T-shirt and jeans. Each of them sported a new pair of Airwalk sneakers. When they walked into rehearsal, we instantly bonded. I had anticipated awkwardness because we were strangers, but instead I found myself jamming with friends. The chemistry was perfect.

We initially spent some time chatting and getting to know one another. Isaac and I spoke first, bonding as guitar players. He seemed to be the most introspective of the three brothers.

Their immediate family accompanied them, and their parents and I spoke a lot as well. Their father, Walker, an executive for an oil drilling company, is a tall, charming man with a friendly manner. He and I discussed music trends and the history and prospects of Hanson. Isaac, or Ike as his family often calls him (his real name is Clarke Isaac), jumped in and out of our conversation. Diana, their mom, was also very friendly. A blanket of blond hair hung down past her waist. I'd never seen such long hair!

The younger siblings were tired from the trip back from Los Angeles, but made themselves known. Mackenzie, the boys' three-year-old brother, who goes by "Mackie", ran all over the place, jumping on and off the stage and screaming his head off while bumping into people and instruments. Jessica, at eight the older of the two younger sisters, asked many questions and checked out everything and everyone. Avery, the six-year-old often called Avie by her family, was very quiet and just hung out drawing pictures. Being the shy one in the family, she occasionally hid behind her mother.

Taylor, who we usually called Tay, although his real name is Jordan Taylor, and I talked about their video shoot, which he described to me

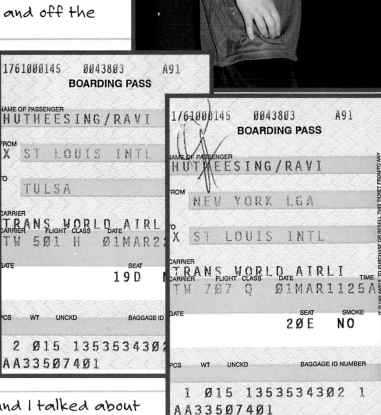

scene by scene. They were all very excited to see the final cut. Zac, who is only called "Zachary" by his parents and only when they want to get his undivided attention, bounced in and out of the conversation, eagerly putting in his two cents worth whenever he could. The Hanson brothers seemed to interrupt one another constantly.

They had also filmed <u>The Jenny McCarthy Show</u>, and everyone was smiling about that, especially Zac. Apparently, Jenny had run up to him to give him a kiss. Zac was pleased that a beautiful woman gave him more attention than she gave his older brothers.

After our get-to-know-you session and a few slices of pizza, con-

tributed by Walker, we began rehearsing "MMMBop." We had rented most of the gear, so it took some time to adjust the equipment to our individual sounds. The guys are all very talented, but Zac initially impressed me the most. He seemed to be more of a natural at his instrument than his brothers. Tay initially banged on his keyboards, making the music sound a bit choppy and heavy. Ike had a harsh sound at first—a tone that was very distorted and metallic. He also had a hard

touch and broke several strings during our first jam session.

The brothers seemed to get along very well, like best friends. They took every opportunity to poke fun at one another. I'm not sure if they had many other friends since they had been home schooled all their lives,

but they may have had friends at church. (The family is Evangelical Christian.) Ike said that most of his peers are home schooled and that home schooling is quite common in Tulsa.

I felt that Zac and I hit it off the best—he was like a little brother and was the least reserved. I found Tay harder to get to know in the beginning. But the more time we spent together, the stronger our friendship became, to the point where I felt closer to him than anyone else in the entire organization. Ike and I also have plenty in common, so we could talk forever.

Tuesday, March 4, 1997—
Tulsa, Rehearsal

We had the morning off, as is often the case, because the boys had school. Our daily schedules usually blocked out time for Walker and Diana to teach their kids all the school subjects. I believe Ashley Greyson, a very close friend of the Hansons, also helped tutor them in math. After an afternoon of rehearsing, we were becoming better friends. We playfully made fun of one another, as good friends do. Zac stumbled on a nickname for me, "Ravioli." I retaliated by calling him "Prozac." By the end of the day, we all had new names.

Zac disliked rehearsing. He tried to establish that every half hour we would take a thirty-minute break. In other words, "Let's not rehearse!" He

I noticed that Zac generally seems to worry: he was worried about Taylor's strained vocal cords and Ike's guitar tone. He also won't try to play anything unless he's sure that he can do it perfectly.

At one point, Tay was practicing a new song that the brothers had written. Zac got up from behind the drums and started banging on the keyboards. Tay kept pushing him away but he would not stop. Eventually Zac said, "Tay, don't play that! Ravi's a songwriter and he might steal it." I did not intend to steal anything, but I was impressed that of all people, an eleven-year-old was most aware of copyrights. He's a sharp little kid!

also went to the bathroom frequently. In fact, we renamed the bathroom "the Zacroom." I think Tay gets the credit for that one.

Zac also tends to wear himself out. He has so much energy most of the time that he nearly collapses when he finally tires out. There is no middle ground. If Tay or Ike talk him into twenty minutes more of rehearsal, he will perform without <u>any</u> energy or enthusiasm.

We had our first meal out together this evening. Ike, Tay, Zac, Walker, Peter Schwartz (keyboardist/musical director), Scott Hogan (bass player), and I went to the Hansons' favorite local spot. It was a fast-food Mexican joint called Taco Bueno. Zac was concerned that we "East Coasters" would not enjoy it. He kept saying, "Uh, I don't think you're gonna like it." They recommended the burritos, which were fine, but more importantly, we had a lot of fun just hanging out together.

Thursday, March 6, 1997—
Tulsa, Rehearsal

Today was hard work. We rehearsed from 10 A.M. to 10 P.M. As Isaac and I did every morning, we went into the side room and jammed together. I wrote out a chord chart for "I Will Come to You," which Ike had a hard time playing. I felt a little weird teaching him his own song! One reason he was having problems with the guitar part was that we had to lower the keys of several songs to accommodate Taylor's changing voice. "MMMBop," "Thinking of You," and "Where's the Love" had all been adjusted. I think Tay strained his voice while recording the album. It was rare that he would sing during rehearsal, and Isaac and Zac usually rested as well. Without the vocals, it was hard to get a feel for how the songs actually sounded.

I sensed a little tension between Peter, our keyboardist/musical director, and the Hansons. He gave us all handouts explaining what his problems with the band were and lectured the brothers on authority and control. He tried to explain that just because they were Hanson, it didn't mean they were experts in making the band sound great. "I have a job to do," he said. "Mercury has asked me to make this band sound a certain way." The Hansons had a lot to learn about making music professionally. We all had to give them time to develop and I wasn't sure that Peter had the patience. I wondered how this relationship would evolve.

Two executives from Mercury Records, Michael Pontecorvo and Steve Greenberg, flew in from New York to check us out. They arrived in the late afternoon and were happy with our sound with one exception—Ike's guitar tone. After Ike made a few adjustments, they were still dissatisfied. I was in a very awkward position because the record label executives asked me to dial up a better tone on his amplifier. I hoped Ike wouldn't hate me for doing that. He must have been humiliated. I did find a sound that everyone seemed to like, except Ike. He was becoming a little angry, and very frustrated. He eventually returned the settings to his original tone.

After the tension dissipated, the record executives took us out for dinner. We all crammed into the Hanson family van and went to a sandwich/deli place. I challenged Zac to come up with the most disgusting combination of foods. Tay happily assisted his little brother. I think they ended up mixing mashed potatoes with chocolate pudding. Fortunately, no one ate it.

Zac jumped me from

behind as I walked out of the restaurant. I gave him a piggyback ride around the parking lot, yelling to everyone that I was taking him hostage.

Friday, March 7, 1997—
Tulsa, Rehearsal

We rehearsed most of the day, and then went out for dinner. This restaurant was a self-serve pizza and Italian buffet place. We sat at a long table in a corner. Tay was in an unusually quiet mood and he spent most of the meal spaced out, staring at a television above my head. When I occasionally asked him a question, he'd nod, smile, or shrug his shoulders in response. That was about all I got out of him. We returned to the rehearsal space and jammed for a couple more hours before we went out to play what we had been planning all week—laser tag.

This was Hanson's favorite game. I had never played before, so Ike, Tay, and Zac promised to help me out. The object is to shoot your laser at an opponent and hit a sensor on his or her vest. If the opponent tags you first, he or she earns points and your gun is inoperable for a few seconds.

We played a few video games in the lobby while waiting for our turn. When our time came, we suited up in a dark waiting room. I slid the vest over my head, grabbed my gun, and was ready for combat. Tay said, "Stick with me!" I figured I'd let him show me the ropes. The doors opened and we all ran in different directions, although I followed Tay up a ramp and backed myself into a corner. I was at his mercy and he fired his laser right at me. So I let loose on him and we chased each other, shooting rapidly. At one point, the Hansons surrounded me and Ike, Tay, and Zac took full advantage of their position. Moments later, Walker decided to join the "attack on Ravi." Okay, no more Mr. Nice Guy! It was my turn to get those blond bullies back. Well, it didn't quite work out that way. They were laser tag pros, so I had to accept defeat. We had so much fun that we wanted to try another round, but the lines were too long. We decided that maybe we'd go again another time before leaving Tulsa, but that never happened.

Saturday, March 8, 1997—
Tulsa, Open rehearsal

This was our last day in Tulsa and we also had our first performance. After a lot of debate, the Hansons decided to have an open rehearsal for their friends and family. About fifty people arrived to check out the band. It turned out to be a fun and relaxed event, but it did not begin that way.

We had major technical problems and began over an hour late. Earlier in the day, our computer had gone down. Peter used it to generate a drum/percussion loop, which played along with the band. The computer also triggered prerecorded backup vocals. While Peter was trying to repair the system, I chatted with the Hansons' friends and relatives. Walker brought some family members up to the stage and asked me to demonstrate my various pieces of gear. I also mingled with some close musician friends of the Hansons. I talked a lot with a local band called the Mellow-Dramatic Wallflowers—now known as Admiral Twin. Apparently, most of Ike's equipment belonged to their guitar player, Brad.

After an unsuccessful attempt to get the computer up and running, we had to perform without technical support. This was a blessing in disguise because we sounded good without it, which was a confidence builder for us all, especially Zac. He realized that he <u>could</u> drive the band without drum loops.

Our show consisted of the five songs that we would perform at our upcoming concert in

We stopped using the prerecorded backup vocals after our first show in Florida.

Florida. The first song was "Thinking of You," followed by "Where's the Love," "Minute Without You," "I Will Come to You," and "MMMBop." After the performance, we rehearsed for another hour and then the crew packed the gear in cases and shipped it all to Florida.

After a week of hard work, the six of us sat on the stage and talked. Tay brought me an original Hanson T-shirt, which I had asked for a couple of days earlier. There is a cartoon picture of the guys on the back and it says "Hanson" across the front. I made a joke about Zac and he playfully picked up the bass player's bag and threw it at me. He didn't realize that there was a solid metal box in the front pocket. It hit me right in the head, causing a little bump to swell. He felt badly about it and apologized to me repeatedly. He's a sweet kid!

Presenting Hanson

Our first show was the National Association of Record Merchandisers convention in Orlando, Florida. NARM is a record company's premier opportunity to showcase a new artist to music retailers. We had to recreate the sound of the Hanson CD, which was why we had eight days of rehearsal for a twenty-five-minute show. We were all very excited about our first road trip as a band, and it certainly was a memorable experience.

Sunday, March 9, 1997—

Tulsa to Orlando

The entire entourage flew from Tulsa to Orlando this morning.

Everyone traveled in coach/economy class. Tay and I sat together and talked about recording Middle of Nowhere.

At present, the brothers, Hanson family, and management travel in **first class**.

They completed it three months earlier, and Mercury would release it in May. He had a CD-R (a reference CD) of the album so we listened to it on the flight.

When we arrived at the Orlando airport, we met Stirling McIlwaine, a smart, young guy and a senior member of Triune Music Group, the Los Angeles-based company that manages Hanson. A van shuttled us all from the airport to our hotel, which was in the Walt Disney World complex. We talked with the bellman and explained who we were and why we were there. He had

never heard of Hanson. That's not surprising because the bellman in Tulsa hadn't, either! I decided to sit by the pool, and soon Isaac, Taylor, Zac, and Walker joined me at my table.

That evening, everyone except the guys from Mercury dined together. Thirteen of us went to a seafood restaurant for a "company dinner." It was a great way to celebrate our first road trip as a band. Taylor and I sat together and we both ordered the same meal—the shrimp platter. Zac sat a few seats away and felt left out of the conversation, so he frequently came to our end of the table to talk. When I wasn't looking, he snagged a couple of popcorn shrimp from my plate. (I guess he was hungry!) Kenny, our production manager, made a nice speech acknowledging everyone's hard work. We also toasted Stirling for taking us out to dinner, but for some reason Walker ended up with the bill! We returned to the hotel after dinner. Everyone wanted to get a good night's sleep before our big show.

Monday, March 10, 1997—
Orlando, First performance

I spent most of the warm, sunny day by the pool. Ike was the first to join me, and we sat around and talked between dips in the pool. He told me that both Tay and Zac were sick. Apparently, sick to their stomachs. The Hansons insisted that it was some form of food poisoning, but I bet that they were just nervous about their first big show. After all, Tay and I had had the same meal and I felt fine!

When Tay, Zac, and Walker arrived at the pool, they joined us at our table and informed us that Peter, our musical director, was also ill. Apparently, he had to go to the emergency room during the night to have a breathing treatment. Could it have been because of the conditions of our rehearsal space for the past week? Tay was feeling a bit better but Zac was still nauseous. After a few hours, they returned to their room to rest.

At 6:30 P.M., it was time to go to the venue. We were performing in the grand ballroom of a nearby hotel. Polygram, the parent company of Mercury Records, had created a party atmosphere and called it the

PGD Zone. It was cool. They had huge TV monitors on the walls and a full bar along one side. Diana and the younger Hansons were already there because they had flown in from Tulsa that day and went directly to the venue.

We did our sound check about an hour later, once Walker and the guys arrived, and everything sounded decent. We then went to our dressing room, which was very large with couches and buffet tables. Dinner was served. Catering is a great benefit in this job, and we had several selections from which to choose. I decided to take a chance and have shrimp again but the Hansons played it safe with turkey sandwiches.

It was time to take the stage. The Hansons all wore polyester sport shirts. Tay was wearing his green one, Zac sported white, and Ike had on a blue and green jacket over his. After the Hansons said a family prayer, we started up the ramp to the stage, where little Mackie grabbed my leg to pull me back. It was so cute. Diana carried him off.

When the guys pick the menu, we usually wind up with fast food, Twizzlers, and Diet Dr Pepper™. They drink diet soda to keep their skin "zit free."

"Here they are . . . Hanson!" said the emcee. The audience of a couple hundred industry-related people appeared skeptical and we were both nervous and excited as we took the stage. As soon as we began, the expressions on the spectators' faces switched to looks of amazement. They obviously could not believe the talent that these three kids possessed. We played with so much energy that the conservative crowd couldn't help but "bop."

We did a great job. I occasionally glanced at the jumbo TV screens to watch us. I think they had a five camera shoot. After our set, we returned to the dressing room where we were greeted ecstatically. People started lining up to meet the guys and have their pictures taken with them. None of us expected this much of a response, but it was obvious that we had stumbled on a formula that worked. Stirling entered the room with a big smile on his face and said that David Letterman wanted to be the first to have Hanson on a late-night talk show. That was exciting news!

The Hansons, except for Isaac, returned to their hotel. He decided to hang out with me and watch a few other bands. I promised Walker and Diana that I would get him back safely.

Our farewell was more emotional than I had expected. Taylor, Zac, and I hugged one another good-bye. This could have been the last time I'd see them, possibly forever. Everyone figured that we would probably soon regroup, but nothing was for sure. I hoped we would because I had so much fun and felt that I'd made some new friends.

Isaac and I watched a few bands and spoke with some industry people. Then we searched the building for his

Ike wearing my sunglasses.

"artist pass," which he had lost. I guess he really wanted to keep it as a reminder of his first professional performance in a band (previously they performed mostly as an a capella group—without instruments). We never found it but we did manage to get another one from the event coordinator. I called a taxi and we went back to the hotel. The next morning, we were all flying back home.

Peter, Scott, and Ike.

Rising to the Top

3

In early April, I received a phone call from Michael at Mercury Records. He asked me, "What are you doing on May 6?" I responded that I had no plans as of yet and asked him what was up. He said, "Well, we're going to do David Letterman and I was hoping you might be available. " Of course, I instantly said yes, knowing that if I had anything planned, I would switch it without hesitating. He said that he would keep me advised as the schedule developed.

We regrouped after a six-week break. Mercury was releasing the CD, *Middle of Nowhere*, and "MMMBop" was climbing the Billboard Hot 100 singles charts. Hanson was on the verge of having a number–one hit.

It was early May when we began promoting the CD. Our first ten days included three major television appearances in New York and a live concert in Los Angeles. The world was about to experience the beginning of "Hansonmania."

Thursday, May 1, 1997—

New York, Rehearsal

For the first time in six weeks, we played "MMMBop" again. In fact, that was all we played for several hours. We were performing on The Rosie O'Donnell Show the next day, and we needed to sound as perfect as possible. The song is three minutes and fifty seconds long, but we needed to reduce it to three minutes flat.

I really enjoyed seeing the Hansons again. Unfortunately, they were very tired from a hectic trip to London. Their schedule was so full that the only way they could make rehearsal was to fly on the Concorde. Isaac, Taylor, and Zac bubbled with fun stories about traveling on the supersonic jet, including the flight statistics (speed, altitude, etc.) and traveling with fellow passenger Puff Daddy.

The executives from Mercury Records attended rehearsal and ordered a mountain of food for us. We all gathered around a big table in the lobby of the rehearsal studio and ate burgers and fries. I met

Hanson's other manager, Christopher Sabec, whom I hadn't met before because he was recovering from major neck surgery.

Following dinner we resumed rehearsing and played "MMMBop" a few more times. After about twenty minutes, Zac started to fade and practically fell asleep behind the drums. It was funny to watch, but I felt sorry for the kid. He was doing a lot for someone of any age!

After rehearsal, the Hansons returned to their hotel and I had an hour's drive home. We all needed to get a good night's sleep before our first network television appearance.

Friday, May 2, 1997—
New York, *The Rosie O'Donnell Show*

A stretch limousine drove up and consumed my entire driveway at around 9 A.M. Not a bad way to go to work! My driver, John, was very cool and told me stories about chauffeuring some of my guitar heroes, like Eric Clapton and Keith Richards. I was proud to join that list as one of his passengers!

VIVEK HUTHEESING

We pulled up to the NBC building and waited for an escort. People gathered around my limousine trying to see which celebrity was inside. I couldn't help but feel that they were in for a disappointment. When the escort arrived, John opened my door and let me out. People started snapping photographs and <u>then</u> tried to figure out who I was. It was weird.

I took the elevator up to Rosie's studio. I had never played at NBC's

studios so I was a bit intimidated. The Hansons hadn't arrived yet so I snooped around, looking at the celebrity pictures on the walls. It was hard to imagine that all these famous people had worked here, and now I would too. I walked onto the <u>Saturday Night Live</u> set. It was cool. <u>I'd like to play on SNL</u>, I thought to myself.

The six of us (Hansons and three sidemen) and the Hanson family relaxed together in a small dressing room. Several top executives from Mercury and Polygram came since Hanson was their biggest act at the time. There was quite a large crowd backstage.

With the Hansons dressed in their usual polyester sport shirts, we were ready to go on. After the family said a prayer, the talent coordinator led us to the stage door where we waited for a couple of minutes. We all slapped high-fives and wished one another good luck.

Inside limousine.

Rosie finished interviewing Gary Shandling and we raced on to the stage during a commercial break as the house band played. I glanced at Rosie and gave her a smile, which she returned with a wink. After strapping on our instruments, we were introduced to millions of viewers by Rosie, who said, "Making their television debut, please welcome Hanson."

Isaac's guitar tone wasn't quite right in the intro, but he quickly fixed it. Tay's voice cracked on his second note, and he seemed to be straining a bit throughout the song. Regardless, we played well and the audience seemed to love it. They were on their feet clapping and swaying to the beat. I had a blast!

Once we had finished "MMMBop," the Hansons went over to talk with Rosie on camera. Zac had some trouble getting there, tripping over his wireless microphone transmitter. They appeared nervous during the interview. Zac was very fidgety, hanging his leg over the armrest of the chair, and speaking in strange voices.

We returned to the dressing room where the vibe was good and everyone felt great about our first television performance. Photographers took pictures of the Hansons with Rosie, and then we descended to the lobby where there were several fans waiting for autographs. The guys signed a few before we got into our limousines.

Tuesday, May 6, 1997—

New York, *The Late Show With David Letterman*

We were at the Ed Sullivan Theater to perform on The Late Show with David Letterman. This show had always been one of my favorites, so I was thrilled to be on it.

We kept messing up "MMMBop" during the sound check because the arrangement was different from the one we had done on Rosie. Each show had different time requirements, so we had to adjust the song length again, playing a three-minute and thirty-second version. Ike kept forgetting the arrangement and strummed his guitar through the vocal break, where only the drums and vocals are supposed to be. Tay became very frustrated. After several attempts, we could only hope for the best, and fortunately, we did it right when it counted.

We had a couple of hours between sound check and the actual performance, so I decided to go outside to visit some of my friends who were coming to see the show. I ran into David Letterman in the stairwell, who seemed nice,

The Ed Sullivan Theater
1697 Broadway
Between 53rd & 54th Streets, NYC
LATE SHOW
with
DAVID LETTERMAN
Tuesday May 6, 1997
PERSONS UNDER 16 NOT ADMITTED

558

Tuesday
May 6, 1997
Doors Close 5:00 P.M.

558

even though he only said, "Excuse me." I also visited a few of the band members from the CBS Orchestra (David Letterman Band), whom I knew from the New York City music scene.

As we had on Rosie, we assembled on stage during a commercial break, following the other guests, who included John Goodman. Ike wore a dark

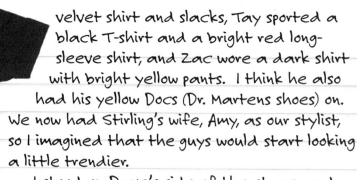

velvet shirt and slacks, Tay sported a black T-shirt and a bright red long-sleeve shirt, and Zac wore a dark shirt with bright yellow pants. I think he also had his yellow Docs (Dr. Martens shoes) on. We now had Stirling's wife, Amy, as our stylist, so I imagined that the guys would start looking a little trendier.

I stood on Dave's side of the stage and he and I exchanged glances and smiles. We started the song and played it quite well, although I think Tay was again straining. I had a great time on stage but Zac didn't look like he was having fun. I asked him why he was so glum afterward and he said he didn't know, but that he did have fun. Maybe he just got that way when he was a little nervous.

When we finished "MMMBop" the spotlight shone on me. Dave came over to me and asked, "Are you a Hanson?" Unfortunately, he caught me off-guard and the only thing I could come up with was "Nah." Everyone heard it.

Following the show, we chilled out in the dressing rooms for about forty-five minutes. I left the building before the Hansons and saw that about fifty people, mostly adults, had

assembled near the stage door waiting for the brothers. I walked out the door and seemed to go relatively unnoticed. All of a sudden, I heard a young voice call my name. I looked up to the sixth floor of the Ed Sullivan Theater and saw Zac and Taylor hanging out a window. I had left my Late Show T-shirt behind and Tay had it in his hand. He threw it out the window and someone on the street caught it and handed it to me. The crowd cheered. Tay went on to yell, "Hey everybody, he's our guitarist! Get his autograph!" After signing about

NIKHIL HUTHEESING

VIVEK HUTHEESING

23

five autographs, I was on my way.

Wednesday, May 7, 1997—
New York, Paramus Mall, New Jersey

Today marked a milestone in the history of Hanson. "MMMBop" had reached number two on the Billboard Hot 100 singles chart, and Middle of Nowhere went gold (over 500,000 copies shipped). Mercury had only released the CD the day before!

We signed Hanson posters to one another at rehearsal. Taylor drew a picture of my guitar and amplifier on mine, and all three of them signed it.

Zac also discovered the double doors leading into the rehearsal studio. In order to get into the studio, we had to walk through one door and then immediately through another. There was about a foot of space in between the heavily padded doors. They designed the entrance this way in order to help sound proof the room. Whenever Zac disappeared, he was usually hiding, sandwiched between the two doors. He would push himself halfway up and wedge himself in place with his foot on the door-knob.

After rehearsal, the Hansons performed an acoustic concert at the Paramus Mall in Paramus,

Walker remarked that as they were driving up and saw crowds of people, he assumed Macy's was having a White Sale!

VIVEK HUTHEESING

Meeting Katie Couric on the Today *show.*

New Jersey. They were only expecting a few hundred people to show up, but the attendance exceeded five thousand.

The crowd response was incredible but the Hansons also got their first taste of how scary life can be as celebrities.

Taylor's shirt was torn and the fans ripped a shoelace out of his shoe. Zac fell and the crowd nearly trampled him. Fortunately, our production manager, Kenny, grabbed him around the waist and carried him out. The experience shook up the Hansons, but at the same time, they seemed to enjoy it.

Saturday, May 10, 1997—

Los Angeles, Sam Goody "in store"

Given the potentially hazardous reaction from the crowd in New Jersey, we took no risks at the show in Los Angeles. A very professional security staff—the same security guards that handle the band U2—were hired by the Hansons to look after us.

We all gathered in the hotel lobby at 9:30 A.M. to board a large van. It took approximately three minutes to get to the Sam Goody store where we were performing. Two police cars escorted us from the hotel to the store's loading dock, which the public could not access, and we entered the building from there. The store hadn't opened yet, but a long line of fans had begun to form outside approximately three hours earlier. Our sound check was difficult because the large empty music store was not good acoustically.

We were all sporting our first official All Access passes.

Because we had them, we could go everywhere while everyone else had limited access. It's like a membership card for a very select club. However, the person who issued the passes screwed up my name and had to write it out by hand.

After a press conference in the upstairs lounge/café area, the six of us took the elevator down to the lower level. Every step of the way we were shadowed by security guards. While the crowd of twenty-five hundred was excited, the fans were very respectful and we were never in any personal danger. The fans screamed so loudly that for the first time in my life, my hearing actually distorted from the sound level. I'd been playing shows for years and had never heard anything like that.

We began with "Thinking of You." It felt so good to play something other than "MMMBop." We then went into "Where's the Love," "Minute Without You," and wrapped it up with the hit.

The show was successful and everyone had a good time. We quickly left the building as the Hansons had to go straight to the airport to return to New York. The rest of us returned to the hotel, had a nice meal at Stirling's house, and then took an overnight flight to New York.

Monday, May 12, 1997—
New York, The *Today* Show

My wake-up call came at 5 A.M. We had arrived the day before from L.A. on the red eye, but fortunately we had most of the day to relax and catch up on our sleep. By 5:45 A.M., we were on the outdoor set of the Today show. It was a cool spring morning and a few Hanson fans had already gathered. Show time wasn't for another three hours!

We did a sound check, and then settled in the green room that most television studios and theaters have. Many of them aren't even painted green! There were all sorts of rolls, pastries and juices so we pigged out waiting to take the stage. Zac and his younger brother and sisters chased one another around the room.

We approached the stage around 8:30 A.M. and were very excited because this was our first live broadcast (Dave and Rosie tape their shows).

Ike, Tay, and Zac did a quick interview with Katie Couric. Zac barely said a word, letting his brothers answer all the questions. I wondered if that was intentional because of how he had behaved on Rosie. After the interview, the Hansons had to move from center stage to their instruments. It was complicated because the show was live and there was no commercial break. Zac kicked a microphone stand, which made a big thump in the homes of millions of people.

Peter, our keyboardist, triggered the computer to start, but Zac was still fumbling with his headset and we had to stop the computer. Taylor stalled by asking the crowd, "Are you ready for this?" We tried again and successfully began "MMMBop." Zac looked a little happier than he had on Letterman, but his headset microphone kept slipping below his mouth and didn't properly pick up his voice.

As we were starting our next song, I realized that Tay had forgotten to transpose his keyboards. I quickly tapped him on the shoulder and pointed to his keyboard. We also played "Where's the Love," but it didn't air on television.

> **T**ay always forgot to make this necessary adjustment to his keyboards after "MMMBop." It became my unofficial job to remind him to do so.

Following the show, the guys posed for pictures, and we briefly returned to the green room to collect our belongings. Most of us elected to walk back to the hotel. The Hansons had a van, but Tay really wanted to walk. Walker was uncomfortable with that for security reasons, although people rarely bothered us on the street. Tay talked his dad into letting him go, and he and the rest of us non-Hansons walked.

> **T**his was probably the last time Taylor walked down a public street without a bodyguard—possibly forever!

4
In the Middle of Everywhere

The promotional tour began in June. Schedules started to change at a moment's notice and we'd fly to cities to make brief appearances and play a few songs. We often traveled long distances in very short time periods.

We began in Los Angeles, where we played a benefit for the Pediatric AIDS Foundation. Our next stop was Detroit and then on to the Hansons' home state, Oklahoma. The second half of the tour was less hectic. We often had a few days to spend at home between trips to Charlotte, New York, Minneapolis, and Los Angeles, where we returned to perform on *The Tonight Show* with Jay Leno. We ended our summer with a fun trip to Toronto, Canada.

From this point on, I was hired by Hanson instead of Mercury. My paychecks were from Hanson Inc., my negotiations were with Triune Music Group, and I rarely interacted with the record company on a business level.

We also had new tour management and crew. For reasons that I may never know, the Hansons released the entourage that had been with us since the beginning. I was disappointed because we really had a good team, but the replacements were also very nice and extremely capable.

However, this unexplained change of personnel sent a little fear through several of us in the Hanson organization. Who would be next? Over the next six months, colleagues would come and go, usually without any explanation. Unfortunately, this became a regular part of Hanson, and things never felt the same.

Friday, June 6, 1997—
Los Angeles, Rehearsal

Early in the morning I had boarded a plane and flew from New York to Los Angeles. Peter, Scott, and I traveled together. Our new head of security, Jason Browning, met us at the gate, and Mark, our new monitor engineer, had just arrived from Dallas. The five of us traveled by van to our hotel in West Hollywood.

We met our new tour manager, Paul Chavarria, who was very charismatic but didn't seem like the kind of guy who could handle such a big

responsibility. We introduced ourselves and he explained the afternoon schedule and told us who was rooming with whom. We were all shocked because we never had to share

rooms before. After our faces hit the floor, he laughed, told us he was kidding, and handed us keys to our private rooms.

As I got to know Paul better, I realized that he is a true professional. His terrific sense of humor, constant practical jokes, and genuine personality, which at first made him seem amateurish, are the attributes that make him a master of his profession.

After settling into my suite, I decided to check out the rooftop pool. It was a nice-sized rectangular pool, surrounded by a patio and several palm trees. There was also a hot tub, and the view from there overlooking Los Angeles was breathtaking. It was like being on vacation! Diana and the three younger Hansons were already sunbathing and swimming.

The guys with Jason, their bodyguard.

Walker, Isaac, Taylor, and Zac arrived from London around 7 P.M. and we rehearsed. They were exhausted so we agreed to keep the rehearsal short. We ran through the same set of four songs that we performed the last time we were in L.A. After about four run-throughs, Zac started to conk out. Isaac slowly drifted into space, making nonmusical noises on his guitar. (He also was doing his Beavis and Butthead impressions, so rehearsal really went downhill!) Taylor was the only Hanson who seemed to be interested and alert. By 10 P.M., we were all on our way back to the hotel.

Sunday, June 8, 1997—
Los Angeles, Pediatric AIDS Foundation benefit

We arrived at a huge private estate near Beverly Hills around 2 P.M. There were celebrities everywhere and plenty of paparazzi at the

entrance. These photographers were very aggressive, climbing over one another to get pictures as they yelled out, "Zac, Isaac, Taylor" to try to get the guys to look toward the cameras. The Hansons handled this well, but I didn't think they were comfortable with it.

Behind the stage was a large pool and pool house, which was our

dressing room area, complete with all the amenities. However, the tasty spread of cold cuts and cheeses was not exactly what the guys wanted, so someone ordered pizza from a nearby parlor. Even the pizzas had toppings that were a bit too eccentric for the Hansons (i.e. mushrooms, green peppers, etc.), but

the guys found some pepperoni, sausage, and plain to devour. (The Hansons are serious meat eaters!)

The show went well. Isaac, Taylor, and Zac elected to do an acoustic set of two songs first—I think they wanted to make the show longer than it had been. They opened with "Madeline" and then played "Man from Milwaukee." After that, the rest of us joined them on the stage and performed the set that we had rehearsed. Scattered across the lawn, the crowd was quiet, but seemed to enjoy the music.

Several celebrities, including Ted Danson, came to say hello after the show. I also spotted Howie Mandel, Adam Sandler, Tyra Banks, and some others. After several hours, we decided to head back to the hotel.

Tuesday, June 10, 1997—
Los Angeles

There was nothing on the schedule for today so I decided to hang out by the pool. Scott, Peter, Zac, Diana, and the younger Hanson siblings were also soaking up some sun. Ike, Tay, and Walker had decided to do something else, but we had fun playing water games and chatting around the pool. Diana asked me if I would work one on one with Ike to help him with guitar parts. I was more than happy to do whatever I could, so I suggested that he come to my room at 5 P.M. It was like taking my teaching career on the road!

Our tour manager had arranged for a sound company to bring a couple of amplifiers to my room. We actually had a nice little setup. Isaac and I worked on "I Will Come to You," which he was still having problems with, but in his defense, it isn't an easy song to play.

We also talked a lot about guitars, studio recording equipment, college, and of course . . . girls! He had many questions and thoughts about all of these subjects. Isaac was very interested in my guitars because I own several custom models—guitars built to my specifications. He liked the idea of having one built specifically for him. The guys were also setting up a studio at home, as well as one that could travel with them, so Ike was inquisitive about my home studio. I also shared my college experience, telling him what I liked and didn't like. Undecided about what he wanted to do when he turns eighteen, Ike was comfortable with a wait-and-see attitude. Our talk eventually got around to girls and he mentioned someone from home that he really liked. He had a sparkle in his eye when he spoke of her. However, being on the road makes it tough to have a relationship, and since he hadn't formally asked her out yet, it might be a while before he could act on his feelings.

As he was leaving my room, he mentioned that the family was going to the house of the president of William Morris (Hanson's booking agency) to see a private screening of the movie The Lost World. He asked me if I wanted to join them and I instantly said yes. He also invited Scott and Peter, but only Scott joined us.

Around 7 P.M. we went to the guy's house. He had a very high-tech screening room with a fully stocked kitchen. There were two levels to sit on with couches on each. The young Hansons all sat on the lower level with Diana and Walker, who were curled up on a couch together. Ike, Tay, Scott, and I all sat in the back and Zac roamed between the two levels throughout the film. The kitchen had a full assortment of candy and soda, and by the end of the film, everyone was on a sugar high. Candy was spilled everywhere. We all pitched in cleaning up, clearing the tables, and rinsing the cans. It was nice to see that Isaac, Taylor, and Zac, despite their celebrity status, were still decent kids with strong values. They were always willing to do their share of the work. I think that their behavior must be a reflection of good parenting.

Wednesday, June 11, 1997—
Los Angeles to Detroit

Diana, Jessica, Avie, and Mackie went home to Tulsa for a few days. The rest of us flew from L.A. to Detroit via Chicago. As we left the first class lounge to go to the gate, paparazzi bombarded us. Isaac put his guitar case on his shoulder, trying to hide his face, and Zac and Taylor jumped to the other side of me. The photographers became obnoxious and started yelling things like, "You guys aren't that big, don't forget what happened to New Kids on the Block!" All of us quickly escaped into the aircraft.

We arrived in Detroit around midnight. One of my cases had been damaged and Walker was missing one of his bags, so he and I went to the baggage service counter to make our claims. Since my heavy suitcase had lost a wheel, Paul, our tour manager, picked it up and tossed it into a wheelchair. I guess that made sense, it was handicapped!

Our trip to the hotel took a long time despite the fact that we were staying right at the air-port. Paul and I started to walk, but the Hansons had piled into a golf cart. Paul and I grabbed on, balancing on the edge of the bumper, as we all putted our way to the hotel. The clock had reached 1 A.M. when the Hansons, entourage, and twenty-five pieces of baggage arrived in the lobby. We were all exhausted. Walker and the boys, strug-gling to keep their eyes open, boarded the first elevator.

Here's a joke: How many Hansons does it take to operate an elevator? For security reasons, the elevators in the hotel required one to put a room key into a slot before (or maybe dur-ing or after) pressing the floor button. Somehow, they just couldn't get the sequence down despite trying what seemed to be every combination of room key and button. They were so tired that all they could do was laugh–Walker was completely slaphappy. It was hilarious to see this family of pop stars crammed into an elevator, going nowhere, and practically on the floor laughing! Eventually the doors closed and that was the last we saw of them for about twelve hours.

Thursday, June 12, 1997—
Detroit, Handleman Convention

We arrived at the venue, a hotel ballroom, and sound checked around 3 P.M. There were many technical problems with the keyboards, and Isaac couldn't find a decent guitar tone. Walker kept telling him to turn his volume down—much like the father of any teenager with an electric guitar!

We returned to the hotel to get dressed and had forty-five minutes to get back to the venue. Then we had only twenty minutes until show time. Ike failed to mention that he had broken a string while practicing back at the hotel. Mark, our guitar technician, could fix it quickly,

except that the small peg that holds the string on the guitar was missing. Ike could only suggest that it might be at the hotel.

Walker sent the driver back to the hotel to look for it. Since it was almost time to take the stage, we had to rearrange the order of the show so the acoustic section would be in the middle of the electric set because the guys didn't want to close the concert acoustically. It was unlikely that the driver would return in time, so Mark searched his creative being for a solution. Without a word he ran outside to some shrubs. Surrounding the bushes were wood chips. He swiped one, came back inside, and using a utility knife, carved a peg. Quite ingenious!

By the time we reached the middle of our show, the driver had come back empty-handed, but Mark had managed to get the guitar working. He was sweating during Isaac's heavy strumming in "Madeline" and "Man from Milwaukee." If that peg had popped out, the string would have gone with it. Fortunately, the make shift peg held.

The crowd, consisting of employees of a distribution company that had sold many copies of <u>Middle of Nowhere</u>, was subdued but clapped politely between songs. Fortunately, a few employees had brought their kids, who occasionally let out a scream.

Following the show, the Hansons did a lengthy autographing session while I mingled with some regional executives from Mercury Records. After an hour, I said good-bye to the Hansons and returned to the hotel. The Hansons finished signing autographs and arrived back at the hotel about an hour later.

Friday, June 13, 1997—
Detroit to Oklahoma City, Frontier City

I went to the breakfast room around 7:30 A.M. because we had an early flight out of Detroit. Isaac, Taylor, and Zac arrived shortly thereafter and we had juice and cereal together. The guys totally zoned out staring at the television. I don't think they even knew what they were watching.

Paul asked us to place our bags outside our rooms by 8:30 A.M. The bellman would pick them up and take them directly to the check-in

counter here at the airport. We littered the hallway with bags, which made me feel like I was on a school field trip. Zac dragged duffel bags twice his size down the hall.

Paul asked me to collect the Hansons' passports and arrive a few minutes early to speed up the process. I got them from Walker, but felt funny running around the airport with Isaac's, Taylor's, Zac's, and Walker's passports. Walker's picture was probably fifteen years old. He looked very different—as if he just stepped off the set of <u>American Bandstand</u>!

When the Hansons arrived at the check-in, Zac asked me, "What gate are we going to?" I replied, "B-11," to which he responded, "Be eleven? I am eleven!"

We boarded a flight to St. Louis, where we would get a connecting flight to Oklahoma City. Again, the Hansons traveled first class and the rest of us traveled coach. The guys all had their schoolbooks with them, planning to turn the front of the plane into a classroom. Sure enough, they were writing papers and solving problems, with their Dad correcting their work. I was amazed that Walker managed to educate his kids while also staying actively involved with every aspect of the band. I believe at this point he was still employed by the oil drilling company as well! We encountered very bad weather and had to circle the St. Louis airport for over an hour. The plane bounced around excessively and I could only see a dark gray sky outside the window. It was scary. My thoughts were with Zac, though, because he had a history of getting airsick! He might have been a bit queasy, but he was all right. We finally landed and had to run through the airport to make it to our connecting flight. The guys had to turn down the few autograph requests from other travelers.

In Oklahoma there was quite a crowd to welcome them—more people than we had seen anywhere else. We made our way to the baggage claim, where I hung out with Tay and Zac while Isaac and the crew hauled cases off the conveyer belt. Kids were coming up to us and asking Tay and Zac for autographs but since Isaac wasn't with us, they had to refuse. The brothers never gave autographs independently of one another.

Peter, Scott, and I boarded a passenger van, the crew boarded a cargo van, and the Hansons and management boarded a luxurious tour bus. We traveled in a motorcade to the hotel, where Diana, the younger Hansons, and the guys' aunt, uncle, and cousins had arrived earlier from Tulsa and were already taking advantage of the large swimming pool. Walker, the boys, and management kept to themselves inside their bus for most of the afternoon.

At 6 P.M., we arrived at Frontier City—the amusement park where we were to perform. The stage was very large and faced a sprawling lawn. Police had contained the excited crowd about a hundred yards away and we did our sound check while the eager fans tried to push past the wooden barricades. Taylor couldn't help but say things such as "How are you guys doing?" through the microphone. This angered Walker and rightly so because people could have been hurt if they got too excited. Kids were already crushing one another against the barricade. Walker reprimanded Taylor and told him to stop. Tay understood, but Isaac and Zac went on to yell into their own microphones! They just didn't get it.

We quickly finished our sound check and then went to hang out in the bus. The Hansons had a bunch of friends at the show who also hung out in the bus with us. Friends of Diana and Walker's brought

Hanging out in the tour bus before the show.

homemade pizzas and cookies for the band. It was a nice gesture, but they didn't realize that we had catering. These same people used to cook food for the Hansons when they performed in backyards! They were still thinking of them as "the kids next door." While we hung out in the bus, the Mellow-Dramatic Wallflowers (Admiral Twin) were on stage warming up the crowd.

Jason, our security guard, handed out new official Hanson All Access passes. These were what we would wear from then on. On the front, there was a picture of the three guys. In red it said "Hanson" and "All Access." We had our names handwritten on the back of our passes. Mine said, "Ravi 'Are You A Hanson?' Hutheesing." I knew that phrase from David Letterman would come back to haunt me!

After consuming burgers and fries, we took the stage. The guys began with the acoustic set and then we all performed the electric. We opened with the usual, "Thinking of You." The overwhelming energy of the fifteen thousand fans enhanced the powerful intro of the song. This was by far our largest audience up to that point and they went wild. The crowd was so dense that I couldn't even see our sound engineer who swore that he was somewhere in the middle. Girls were fainting and guards had to carry them out to ambulances. It was quite a scene and the show was a huge success.

As usual, we all just strolled off the stage after the closer. Paul grabbed Isaac, Taylor, and Zac and pushed them back onstage to take a bow. They were a bit ambivalent, but they bowed anyway. Stars-in-training, I guess.

We returned to the tour bus, and within minutes all three brothers were engrossed in a Jim Carrey movie. They had completely tuned out anything and

Ashley Greyson, the Hansons' close friend/coworker/tutor, seated in the back lounge of the tour bus at the end of the hallway lined with twelve bunk beds, writing our names on the All Access passes.

anyone around them. I was amazed. How could they walk off a stage after such a big show and zone out as if nothing had happened? Walker asked them repeatedly to brush their hair and get ready to do an autograph signing, or as we call them, a "grip and grin," which essentially means a quick handshake and smile.

After repeated requests, the guys hadn't moved away from the TV, forcing Walker to do a very fatherly thing. He went right up to the television, said, "That's it," and turned it off. Within minutes the guys were signing thousands of posters, CD covers, and T-shirts.

I interrupted the Hansons, said good-bye, and returned to the hotel. About an hour later, the Hansons wrapped up the "grip and grin" and traveled home to Tulsa in the tour bus with all their friends and family. The next day I was heading back home for a few days.

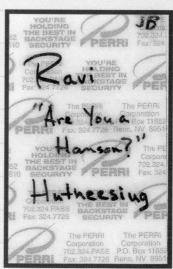

Thursday, June 19, 1997—
Charlotte, Outdoor Concert

We arrived at the venue around midday for a sound check. It was in an outdoor courtyard in front of a bank, and the sun beating down on us made it incredibly hot. A member of our crew brought three bottles of water to the stage, one each for Ike, Tay, and Zac. Taylor glanced at me after taking a sip of his water and asked, "Don't you want some water?" I said, "Yeah, but I'm sure they will bring it in a second." Taylor put his bottle down, ran off the stage and went to the cooler. Seconds later he returned with three bottles of water for the rest of us onstage. That is very characteristic of Taylor. He is considerate of others and a sincerely generous person. I don't know too many other people his age who exhibit so much kindness and decency.

There were already several hundred fans in front of the stage. After a couple of hours, we went back to the hotel for quick showers and when we returned to the venue, rowdy fans were everywhere. We all—including Diana and the younger kids, who had joined us in Charlotte—spent a lot of time hanging out in our dressing room, which was a conference room in the bank. The usual amenities covered the large table—Diet Dr Pepper™, potato chips, and Twizzlers. (Although, to everyone's disappointment, the Twizzlers were strawberry flavored!)

Ike and I struck up a conversation about anti-frizz hair spray—not a very guy-like thing to discuss! He asked me if I was going to grow my hair out and I said that I wanted to but that it always got too frizzy.

He gave me a few pointers.

When we took the stage, the Hansons first played the acoustic versions of "Madeline" and "Man from Milwaukee" by themselves. The eight thousand fans went wild when we started into the electric set, but what was exceptionally cool was that among the "I Love Tay" and "Hanson Rules" signs was a banner that said, "Hi, Ravi." I hadn't seen that before!

After the concert, the Hansons held a "grip and grin" inside and people were lining up outside where I was chatting with some friends. A girl came up and asked me to sign her ticket. I complied. Then another girl came up and asked the same thing. Before I knew it, a crowd of people had formed around me. I was signing tickets, shirts, hats, hands, or whatever they wanted. I was flattered and it was a lot of fun. The local security guards were concerned about the large gathering of people because I was sitting on a wall with my back to a bush and fans were sneaking up behind me. The crowd was getting a bit out of hand and in order to preserve security, I had to start declining requests. Ever since that day, I have made a point to spend some time with the fans.

Thursday, June 26, 1997—
New York, *Fox After Breakfast*

A car collected me at 6:30 A.M. It wasn't easy getting up that early, considering that I had arrived home from the previous day's rehearsal only four hours earlier. It was a relatively peaceful ride into Manhattan until the driver decided to gripe about how much he hates his job. I just sat there and listened.

I was surprised to see that the stage at <u>Fox After Breakfast</u> was a cordoned-off area on the sidewalk. Everything seemed cluttered and disorderly. I badly needed a cup of coffee so I headed straight for the green room. The security guard said that I had to get a pass from the front desk. For some reason, the desk did not have my name on any list,

MIKE CONTI

and no one would give me my credentials. Fortunately Christopher, our manager, arrived and took care of it immediately.

Both of my brothers and a few friends had come by to watch the show live. I decided to hang out with them outside on the sidewalk, while other guests, including Peter Fonda, did segments. We chatted for a while and I greeted some of the fans, signed autographs, and posed for pictures. After about forty-five minutes, I was summoned upstairs to join the gang, but we turned around immediately to go back down to the stage.

The show's hosts interviewed the guys, and this time Zac answered a few of the questions. Ike started to ramble a bit, stumbling on a couple of questions. We then played a two-minute-and-thirty-second version of "MMMBop," lowering the key even further to ease the strain on Taylor's voice. We

screwed up the arrangement after the first chorus, but somehow got back on track and finished the song correctly. After a commercial break, we closed the two-song concert with the TV debut of "Thinking of You." The show was lots of fun, but it was incredibly hot. By 8:30 A.M., it was already above ninety degrees! Despite the sweltering conditions, the crowd of a couple of hundred loved the performance and cheered us on.

We returned to the dressing room to cool off. I invited my friends and family to join us and introduced them all to the Hansons. After fifteen minutes they left and I joined the guys on the set of Access Hollywood. They were doing a quick interview. I had the rest of the day

off, so I rejoined my friends and spent the day
with them. The Hansons had a busy day of photo shoots and press.
<u>Entertainment Weekly</u> booked them all afternoon to do a photo shoot in
the "meat packing" district in lower Manhattan. Following that, they
were scheduled to spend the late afternoon at Coney Island doing an
interview with <u>Rolling Stone</u>. Later in the evening, a limousine drove me
to a hotel in New Jersey.

Friday, June 27, 1997—
<u>New York to Minneapolis, WPLJ, Jam for Hunger</u>

When I arrived at the Meadowlands complex in New Jersey at 5 A.M.,
there was already a long line of people waiting to get into our show.
Apparently, kids <u>and</u> their parents had started lining up at midnight! We
weren't performing until 8:30 A.M.

The Hansons arrived an hour later and we all ate breakfast together. It was another hot morning so we moved into an air-conditioned trailer. Tay and I compared our Dr. Martens—we both have red rub-off
(dark red and black splotched) boots, although his are a little higher
cut than mine.

At show time, we rocked! We performed under a large yellow and
red tent that sheltered several thousand fans from the blazing sun. I
can't believe how much energy the band had at that hour of the day.
The crowd of about three thousand was unbelievably loud while we
performed our usual set. After the concert, we ran off the stage and
straight into a van; we had a plane to catch.

We arrived in Minneapolis and went directly to the concert site
where we were performing that evening. The venue was a parking lot

outside the Mall of America on a very large stage overlooking a sea of about ten thousand seats. Fans were anxiously lining up at the entrance gate hoping to catch a glimpse of the guys. The Hansons started selling T-shirts at this

show, and were raking it in on a batch of brown and green shirts. I asked Stirling if I could have a T-shirt and he replied, "You can if you want, but can you fit into a large junior?" They had only manufactured children's sizes!

In the back was a large tented area with catering. It was a perfect place to hang out, especially since Diana and the kids had joined us there. We all spent a lot of time together kicking balls and having fun while a comedian warmed up the crowd. I thought he was funny, but the crowd wanted Hanson and booed him off the stage.

When it was time to rock, we did! The band was getting tighter and tighter and the fans had a blast as usual.

After a morning concert in New Jersey, a flight to Minneapolis, and an evening show, we were all slaphappy. We brought several large inflatable balls onto our minibus. On the way to the hotel, which we hadn't even checked into yet, we tossed them around and batted them at one another. Even Walker joined in the fun! The bus had long metal poles hanging from the roof and Zac climbed them and kicked the

balls at the rest of us. We were laughing hysterically while pounding them as hard as we could. At the same time we were barreling down the high-way, not to mention that half the entourage had fallen asleep despite occasionally being hit by a missed hit ball.

We initially failed to notice a long line of cars following our bus, which was becoming a familiar sight after leaving a venue. Since our hotel was far from the Mall of America, we didn't expect them to follow us all the way. It isn't easy to lose anyone in a minibus either!

A single guy was in the car directly behind us. We were used to seeing moms with their teenage daughters, but this

Comedian warming up the crowd.

was not a typical fan. Who knew what his motive was? Child celebrities occasionally receive kidnap threats, so one can't be careful enough. We all continued to act rather silly despite the potential seriousness of our situation. Walker paused from the ball bashing and took out his video camera. In our playful frame of mind, we challenged one another to read the car's license plate while Walker zoomed in on it. Finally Taylor was able to read the number, which Walker confirmed.

The guy followed us back to the hotel, along with people in several other cars. Jason got out of the van and approached the vehicle. He and the driver exchanged a few words while the rest of us sneaked into the hotel. Apparently, the guy only wanted an autograph, as did the oth-ers who had followed us. They all wound up going home empty-handed.

Saturday, June 28, 1997—
Minneapolis, rained-out show

We were to perform a show with several other bands. It was an odd gig because the stage was in the parking lot of a bar—not a typical venue for a Hanson concert.

We left for the venue several hours late because of the weather. The trip to the parking lot took an hour, so to pass the time, we played an alphabet game. Someone says, "My mother went to the grocery store and she bought an APPLE." Then the next person says, "My mother went to the grocery store and she bought and APPLE, and BUBBLE GUM." The object is to add on a product each time in alphabetical order. If you skip a letter or forget a product, you lose. Zac wasn't very good at this game but he got a bigger kick out of watching everyone else play. Taylor didn't want to play initially, but he eventually conceded and lost early. Ike missed around "M." It eventually came down to a grueling match between Walker, Jason, and me. Walker eventually lost, leaving Jason and me to duel it out. We completed the entire alphabet and started repeating the letters. Once we arrived at the venue, we agreed to resume the game after sound check. David, a reporter from Entertainment Weekly, was also traveling with us during our stay in Minneapolis. He was observing us, and always taking notes on how the Hansons acted on the road, for a feature article that he was writing. I remarked to him that I hoped he was being paid by the word. It seemed as if he had documented our entire game!

JOHN "RATSO" GERARDI

It had rained so hard that the waterlogged plywood stage was beginning to warp and the ground was very muddy. The generator that powered our equipment was literally swimming in a pool of water. We did a quick, lousy sound check and everything sounded horrific. This gig was heading for disaster.

We boarded the bus and traveled back to the hotel. I eventually beat Jason at the alphabet game when he missed on the letter P on the second go-round. Everyone wanted to play again so we started a new game, which I won when Jason stumbled on the letter W. My competitors officially crowned me "alphabet king."

We arrived at the hotel with enough time for a few hours of rest. Christopher had arranged a big lunch for us in the hotel dining room. After we stuffed ourselves, the Hansons had a press conference with the reporters from Latin America that lasted about an hour. I retreated to my room and flipped on the TV. There were warnings of tornadoes in our area. Despite the pouring rain and gale-force winds, we piled back into two vans and began a hair-raising journey to the venue. The Hanson family went in one van, and the management, label executives, the reporter from Entertainment Weekly, Peter, Scott, and I went in the other. The weather was so bad that several times we had to pull over to the side of the road until the rain subsided. We tried to contact Paul (the tour manager), who was all by himself in the minibus. He had to go to the airport to arrange tickets for the Hansons' night flight and never made it back to the hotel. His plan was to go directly to the venue. Eventually, we reached him and he suggested that we all meet up at a gas station and figure out what to do. That was fine except somehow we needed to get that message to the Hansons. It wasn't easy because they didn't have a cell phone. Meanwhile, there were three phones in our van. Poor planning for sure!

We tried to flag them down through our window, but visibility was poor and they couldn't see us. Every time we rolled down the window, buckets of rain splashed inside. We finally managed to attract their attention and everyone, including Paul, pulled into a gas station simultaneously.

Paul got out of his bus, and Stirling got out of our van. They were going to discuss a plan of action. The Hansons' van had parked in between the other two vehicles, and somehow when Paul ran to us and Stirling ran to Paul, they passed each other on opposite sides of the Hanson van. It was very funny to watch as each of them arrived at the other's vehicle, looking very serious.

Eventually after a lengthy debate, they decided to cancel our appearance. For some reason, amidst the confusion, Walker had the urge to start taking pictures. Isaac, Taylor, Zac, Peter, Scott, and I were

huddled under an overhang, smiling for the camera. Meanwhile a raging storm was in full progress all around us. It was actually a lot of fun. What we didn't realize until later was that the backdrop in the pictures was the station's slogan, "Formula for the Future." How appropriate! Others seeking shelter from the storm recognized us and pulled into the gas station. The market in the station did a great business in selling disposable cameras, and customers started snapping pictures of us, capturing a very memorable "offstage" Hanson moment.

After the impromptu photo session, the Hansons went directly to the airport to fly back to Tulsa. The rest of us went to the venue to collect the crew who had been out in this terrible weather all day. At this point Mark, the technician/stage manager who had fixed Ike's acoustic guitar in Detroit, informed us that he was leaving the group to go with another band. Again, we would have to take on new personnel.

We realized that the Hansons had left some luggage in our van, so we detoured to the airport and dropped it off. Since we didn't have proper good-byes at the gas station, we all hung out for a little while.

Christopher and I flew to New York together the next morning. He and I had never had a chance to get to know each other before. During our flight, I learned what a terrific guy he is, and how he stuck to his vision and made Hanson a hit despite the many roadblocks that he encountered.

Christopher was practically the laughingstock of his law school friends in Atlanta when every major record label, including Mercury Records, turned Hanson down. However, he didn't give up and after

Christopher shared the story of how he first discovered the guys, when they approached him in a parking lot at a music festival in Austin, Texas. Not knowing who they were, and the Hansons not knowing who he was, one of the brothers (he couldn't recall which one) asked if they could sing for him. He agreed and after listening to them, all he could say was, "Where are your parents? I need to talk to them fast!" After giving up his law practice and negotiating a management deal with the family, he had a vision for Hanson that eventually turned into a reality.

approaching Mercury with Hanson's second independent CD (he had initially been shopping the band with their first) he sealed the deal.

When we arrived at the airport we collected our luggage and met our drivers. He gave me a friendly hug and we went our separate ways.

Thursday, July 10, 1997—
Los Angeles, *Weird Al Show*, Drive by

I arrived in L.A. last night so I would be well rested for an early start today. At 8:30 A.M., a limousine transported Peter, Scott, and me to the NBC studios, where we would tape the Weird Al Show. Most of the crew for this leg of the tour were locals, who weren't familiar with our gear, so setting up was harder than usual.

The Hansons arrived soon after and we performed "Where's the Love." We ran it several times because we didn't play it perfectly any single time. The director finally asked us to repeat just the ending so they could edit it together with the previous version of the song. We did as they asked, but Zac let his hair down in between takes. Therefore, if they edited the segments together, his hair would be up for most of it and down at the end, which wouldn't look right. Taylor tried to convince Zac to re-tape the end with his hair up, but he insisted on keeping it down, forcing us to redo the entire song. The director of the show was not pleased with the amount of time we were taking, but we did it over anyway.

During the taping, the band INXS dropped by to check us out. They were performing on the Jay Leno show in the studio next door. After we finished our taping, the Hansons acted out a skit with Weird Al and we all returned to the hotel.

After a few hours off, Scott and I hopped in a car and went to rehearsal. The Hansons arrived about three hours later. We rehearsed "Where's the Love" a few times and then ordered in a big Chinese dinner. Mark Hudson, who co-wrote four of the songs on Middle of Nowhere, including "Where's the Love," joined us for the dinner.

We had heard that a radio station was sponsoring a ticket giveaway at a nearby park. Apparently, they were giving away tickets to our appearance on <u>Jay Leno</u> the next day to the person with the largest Hanson sign. We decided after dinner to get into the van and go check it out. Because the van had tinted glass, no one would be able to see us.

When we arrived at the park I couldn't believe the scene. There were people everywhere with enormous signs. Radio deejays were walking around with microphones. It was wild to be there, one layer of tinted glass separating us from fans who would have loved to catch a glimpse of the guys. We circled around twice and the second time, a few people pointed. Obviously they noticed that a white van with tinted windows was circling. We turned on the radio to hear the live coverage of this scene.

One of us suggested opening the sliding door and waving. This created quite a debate because it could have become a security hazard. As we circled the second time, we discussed how we would do it. On the third approach, Paul (the tour manager) got out and informed the police of our plans. Once he had notified all the officials, he came back to the

van and opened the sliding door. Someone started to roll the videotape (which appeared in <u>Tulsa, Tokyo, and the Middle of Nowhere</u>) and Oscar, our driver, started to drive very slowly. Paul was yelling, "Slow down" because people were coming into the street and he was afraid that we might run someone over. The fans went crazy. I couldn't believe the hysteria. At one point it looked as if things were going to get out of control. Paul jumped back in the van and yelled, "Get out of here!" As we pulled away, people ran into the street chasing us. It was amazing.

The whole time the radio jocks were giving a play-by-play account of what we were doing. It was so strange to be sitting in the van with the guys while listening to a deejay on the radio say things like, "I can see Zac in the front seat leaning out the window waving to the fans!"

The consensus was that the drive-by was successful and a great thing to do for the fans. As we drove away, the radio deejay said something like, "Isaac, Taylor, and Zac—you gave your fans something they will never forget."

On the way back to the hotel, "Where's the Love" came on the radio. I think that was the first time any of us had heard it on the air. It is always special when you first hear your song on the radio and I was fortunate enough to witness this in the company of the Hansons and Mark Hudson!

Friday, July 11, 1997—
Los Angeles, *The Tonight Show with Jay Leno*

We returned to the NBC studios this morning at 9:30 A.M. to prepare for The Tonight Show with Jay Leno. I was beginning to feel like a regular on TV. Once the Hansons arrived, we ran a sound check and then relaxed together in the dressing rooms. Diana spent much of the time braiding Zac's hair for the show. For Jay's interview, the guys were asked to come up with the strangest question that anyone had ever asked them. We tossed around several options and came up with, "How did you guys meet?" They also had to think of a funny story to share. Ike decided to play a trick on the host by pretending that he had dented Jay's white Jaguar in the parking lot.

Jay Leno dropped by our dressing room to say hello. He seemed like a very nice guy, chatting with us and making jokes. Diana happened to be in the bathroom when he arrived, so Jay stood outside the door yelling things like, "Hi, Mom! Just stopped by to see how you were doing! Everything okay?"

I decided to sit in the studio audience for a while and watch Jay rehearse. It was fun seeing him and his staff perfect jokes and bits. When the audience arrived, I chatted with some of the fans. Several told me that NBC wouldn't allow some of their friends in because they were less than sixteen years of age. I actually did see ushers checking the IDs of some kids. In fact, the network was so strict about the age policy that many kids protested outside the studio doors.

After Jay completed interviews with Howie Mandel and a four-year-old genius, we took the stage behind a closed curtain. We slapped high-fives and did our thing. We sounded good, belting out a tight version of "Where's the Love," although Zac seemed to be having problems singing the high notes and didn't smile much during the tune. This was the first time we had played that song on television (Weird Al wouldn't air for several more weeks). At the end of our performance, Ike came over and gave me a high-five. When I watched it later on TV, I could almost see it as he walked over to Jay's desk for the interview. I was surprised that Ike did that because he generally does not acknowledge anyone on stage. I suppose we bonded during the guitar section in the middle of "Where's the Love" when we both looked at each other and strummed in sync.

Jay interviewed the guys after our performance. Unfortunately, Ike's story about Jay's car didn't work as well as he had hoped. His delivery wasn't right.

When it was time to leave, Isaac, Taylor, and Zac decided to go out and wave to the fans who were protesting because they were not allowed into the show. I decided to tag along to see what it was all about. The underage crowd really appreciated the Hansons taking the time to say hello. It's nice that Isaac, Taylor, and Zac really care about their fans.

I walked out to our limousine to meet Scott and Peter. They were not there but a crowd of girls was. I chatted with them and signed autographs. Peter and Scott soon showed up and we all went back to the hotel. That night, I went out to dinner with Paul (tour manager), some members of Triune Music Group, and Amy (stylist). We planned to go see INXS in concert after, but never made it. The Hansons decided to rent some movies and order room service to their suite. They were very kind and invited me, but I figured that I'd take this opportunity to check out the concert. On my way down to the lobby, I stopped off at their room to say good-bye, as I would not see them again for a while. They were headed to Asia for a monthlong press tour.

Friday, August 15, 1997—
Toronto, Rehearsal

   Again, we had a mostly new crew so our technical setup was cumbersome. Paul Chavarria had left us to manage Fleetwood Mac's new tour. His wife, Patricia, took over his duties and started traveling with Hanson. Fortunately, she is incredibly competent as well and a very nice person.
   We had an interesting rehearsal. For the first time ever, the Hanson brothers began to throw some weight around in the band. They seemed to have a definite agenda of what they wanted to accomplish and in what order they were going to do it. They appeared to be taking over the role of musical director. I felt that the tension between the guys and Peter was increasing, and Isaac, Taylor, and Zac were starting to make creative decisions without consulting him. The fact was that they were selling records, and that did put them in the driver's seat on many issues. I knew this wouldn't go over well with Peter but for better or worse, the Hansons were going to control the direction of this band.

Our rehearsal space in Toronto.

Saturday, August 16, 1997—
Toronto, YTV *Psykoblast*, Riding the roller coasters

We got to the venue, Paramount Wonderland Park, around 2:30 P.M. The stage for our live Canadian television broadcast was cool! In front of

the stage were thousands of seats under a shell, all surrounded by lawn.

Scott and I thought we would take in a few rides before the show. However, there wasn't enough time so I spent most of the afternoon with the Hansons.

The 17,000 fans went wild when we took the stage—our sound engineer clocked the noise level at

one hundred forty decibels, equivalent to the noise on an aircraft carrier! We played the usual set and the show was a great success. We'd never sounded so good.

Following the show, the park officials arranged for us to go on some rides. Ike, Tay, Zac, Walker, Jessica, Jason (our body-

guard), four park attendants, and I climbed aboard a van and were driven from ride to ride. The attendants held up the lines at each one, so we

could enter through the exits to get the best seats. The privileges of Hanson! Fans were going crazy as they watched us jump onto roller coasters. Walker captured the entire experience on video. It was awesome!

The first ride was Drop Zone, a free fall from very high up. Zac, Jessica, and I chickened out, but Ike, Tay, and Walker went. There was room for one more, and Taylor begged me to join them. I was about to give in when Jason saved me by going.

The next rides were the roller coasters. We rode several different types—a wooden one, a couple of high-tech corkscrew and loop coasters, and a stand-up one.

Isaac, Taylor, and Zac decided to bungee jump. Wow! I couldn't handle that so I remained grounded. Zac didn't want to go either, but his big brothers talked him into it. It was very cool because the three of them jumped together, creating an amazing moment for the crowd below. What a sight! Walker captured it on video and they used it in Tulsa, Tokyo, and the Middle of Nowhere. As they were swinging overhead, you could hear me screaming, "Yeah!" After all the excitement, we drove back to our hotel talking about all the fun we'd had.

Saturday, August 23, 1997—
New York, Arthur Ashe Kids Day Show

At 9:15 A.M., a limousine arrived at my house to take me to perform our first stadium concert at the Arthur Ashe Kids Day in Queens, New York. The driver was supposed to have concert tickets for my family, but he knew nothing about them. The traffic was heavy as we

approached the stadium and the police were no help in expediting my arrival.

I asked the driver to let me out on the street as I was already twenty minutes late and figured it would be faster to go by foot. I cut through several parking lots and hopped a fence. Fortunately, everything except my guitar was already on site so maneuvering was simple.

When I approached the stadium VIP entrance, I noticed a crowd of excited girls blocking my way. They took many pictures and asked for autographs. I signed a few but had to decline most of them in the interest of time.

When I finally got to the stage,

I found out that the Hansons hadn't arrived yet! I was so agitated. Furthermore, the tickets that I had reserved for my family, which I assumed would be at the stadium since my driver did not have them, were not there. I was

totally frustrated.

The Hansons finally arrived and were in worse moods than I was. They didn't say hello to any of us. They marched on the stage and we did a sound check, which Ike grumbled all the way through. Then they disappeared. I finally found Stirling and inquired about the tickets that I had requested. He had them in his pocket and handed me four, leaving me to figure out how to get them to my family. I contacted the promoters directly and made arrangements to keep the tickets at a location my family could access.

We divided the show into three sets, starting with "MMMBop." I tried going back to check on my family after we finished a good-sounding version of the song. Security had already whisked the guys offstage and into a private dressing room, but for some reason, the rest of us had to confront the crowds alone. It wasn't easy, as there were many excited girls screaming and crushing in on us.

I eventually managed to get into the dressing room and found the security guards hassling my family. Apparently, no one bothered to tell them that my family had tickets and were sitting in the box seats designated for band guests. After confirming the identity of my family, I introduced them to the Hansons, who were extremely polite. However, security said that they had to relocate my family to other seats. The guards brought them to the far side of the

57

stadium, where it was difficult for me to go without an escort, not to mention that now they had a lousy view of the stage.

We returned to the stage to perform "Where's the Love," and then completed the show with the full four-song set. None of us smiled onstage. The guys again hurried off the stage follow-

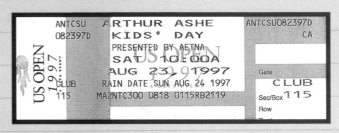

ing the performance. No one said good-bye, "good job," or made any of the customary acknowledgments.

I eventually got to our dressing room after pushing through the crowd. Almost everyone had gone. When the crowd dissipated, I was able to find my family but my limousine was nowhere in sight. After several telephone calls, a car arrived to take my mother and me home. Our show was good, but that was one of the few with Hanson that I prefer to forget.

5

Documenting Hanson

This was one of the most stressful periods that we had. For the first time, I felt that the brothers had changed, and were acting less friendly toward everyone. Ike was the worst, rarely saying hello or good-bye to anyone. Taylor and Zac just kept to themselves. They were constantly late to rehearsals, if not blowing them off entirely, and didn't seem to care much about the music or any of us. Fortunately, this change was only temporary.

Directors, record company executives, agents, parents, and management pulled at them from every angle, putting them under great pressure. This caused growing tension among everyone in the Hanson organization.

We rehearsed for three days prior to filming the concert portion of the documentary. During this time, Hanson nearly made several amateur decisions that would have violated the rights of the rest of us. I think that was a problem with them: they got too big, too fast, and missed learning the protocol of the business.

Monday, August 25, 1997—
New York, Rehearsal

I arrived on time for our 3 P.M. rehearsal and was surprised to find recording apparatus in the room. I asked our engineer what was going on, and he informed me that the Hansons wanted to record us jamming to use as background music for the upcoming long-form video. "Hmm, interesting," I thought to myself. They were planning to tape us, release the recording commercially, and pretend that today was only a rehearsal. In the professional world, that was a commercial recording. I would have expected to receive a contract and a recording fee.

The Hansons strolled in at 7:30 P.M. without even acknowledging that they were over four hours late! Furthermore, they got on the telephone for a half hour before we started making music. For some reason, they opted not to record rehearsal and wrapped things up by 9 P.M. I couldn't believe that I had spent the entire afternoon there and we accomplished next to nothing. The good part was that I didn't have to confront the recording issue. Nevertheless, this whole project was losing focus and the Hansons didn't seem to care anymore. If <u>they</u> didn't care, what was the point?

Wednesday, August 27, 1997—
New York, Beacon Theater dress rehearsal

I arrived at the theater by 5 P.M., just in time for dinner break. Why did they always ask me to arrive at the most useless times? Fortunately, everyone seemed more relaxed and friendly today, and the Hansons and I enjoyed sitting down to a meal together in the auditorium.

Stirling asked me if I wanted tickets for tomorrow's show. Of course, I did, but I had asked about them a week ago. Now I needed to try to get friends to come at such short notice. I did manage to use ten tickets, and reluctantly invited my mother and brother, hoping that this would be a better experience than their last Hanson show.

Christopher came up to me with a stressed expression on his face. I had a feeling we were about to get into a negotiation on the video release form and my compensation. However, when I asked him what was up, he simply stated, "I just found out that we are the number-one-selling band in the

world." I gave him a high-five and a congratulatory hug. He was a big part of that success story.

We rehearsed the show, tested camera angles, and spent a load of time just hanging around. Jason also distributed new All Access passes to each of us. These were similar to our other ones, but the writing was in green and instead of All Access printed across on it, it said, "Middle of Everywhere."

When we finally completed the tasks, I hopped on a train and went home, knowing that first thing tomorrow I had to come right back.

Thursday, August 28, 1997—
New York, Beacon Theater

My call at the Beacon Theater was 12 P.M., despite having a late rehearsal last night and having to commute. I raced to get there from home, which is about an hour's journey by train. However, when I arrived, nothing was on schedule and I sat around for hours. I didn't know why that still surprised me. Things like that happened all the time!

We spent a lot of time backstage, and had a great meal and many good conversations. The Hansons were very busy and everyone bombard-

ed them with questions about the shoot. They had also flown in the entire family and about ten friends from Tulsa to share in the event.

Many members of William Morris and Mercury attended the taping, as did many friends of Hanson. This was a major event for the band. After only six months of public awareness, we were shooting a documentary!

I was very tense all day, waiting for some-one to stick a video release form under my nose. However, no one addressed the issue until we got to the stage entrance about ten minutes before the taping. Stirling came up to me and said, "Hey, you need to sign this or they won't let us start!" I was annoyed because I felt that the proper thing would have been to give it to me in advance, let my attorney review it, and then allow me to submit it. I refused to sign it on the spot. The executives from Mercury Records acknowledged my rights and allowed us to start without my signed document. I submitted the release the following week after my attorney reviewed it and made a few changes.

The show went extremely well and the beautiful architecture and structural detail of the theater was the perfect setting for this momentous event. We performed two identical sets, which were recorded by a mobile studio in a truck parked outside. The directors would select the best of each set and compile them as one performance.

Tay made a speech on stage that made little sense, although what he was trying to say was clear. However, it become a regular part of our show from then on, and he usually phrased it in the same way every time. "Okay guys, you're at a Hanson concert. There's no rules. The only rule is that you cannot stand still. You have to have fun. You have to go crazy. And you can't be here if you are not having fun."

After the show, I was ready to leave, but decided to wait for the Hansons to finish shooting the video for "I Will Come to You." They did a "live concert" video for the song, although they lip-synched to the prerecorded music. However, they ended up not using the footage.

Later that evening, they were going to Europe for an extensive press tour and I wouldn't see them for a couple of months. When they finished taping, they were in such a rush to get to the airport that I almost missed them altogether. Taylor noticed that I was still there and came over to say good-bye. Ike followed suit, but Zac slipped into their van. I don't think he saw me standing there. I waved them off and then joined a few of my friends for dinner.

Our trip across the country had tightened up the band. We had perfected our live show and were no longer just a one-song television act. The autumn season included visits to Chicago, Los Angeles, Miami, Kansas City, and Atlanta. Diana and the younger Hansons didn't join us in any of those cities, except L.A.

With the video shoot behind us, some of the internal tension had dissipated. However, just when we thought we were stable our personnel changed again, and this time, it wasn't just among the crew. Consequently, we had some of the most disorganized and disastrous shows ever.

Wednesday, October 29, 1997—

Chicago, Rehearsal – First listening of *Snowed In*

After training our mostly new crew, we spent ninety-eight percent of the day's rehearsal working on "I Will Come to You." Ike and I hung out in the lobby with our guitars going over the parts. Peter worked with Taylor on keyboards, and Zac sprawled out on the floor behind his drums reading Lego™ magazines. It wasn't the most productive rehearsal, but we were determined to start playing the ballad, which we hadn't performed in seven months. There was a lot of official business going on in

the other room. Walker and Patricia were discussing possible performances including one at the White House.

When we weren't rehearsing "I Will Come to You," we hung out talking. The guys played some of the cuts off their CD-R of *Snowed In*. We listened to "Little Saint Nick," "Merry Christmas Baby," and "At

Christmas." Ike and I actually started strumming through "At Christmas" for the fun of it.

We also had a long discussion about our last names. Isaac explained that originally their last name was H-a-n-s-e-n, which he said is the Danish spelling. However, when an ancestor of theirs came to America many years ago, he mistakenly spelled it H-a-n-s-o-n. Now everyone thinks that the family is Swedish!

They were very interested in my last name. I explained the origin of Hutheesing and I was amazed at how well Isaac, Taylor, and Zac were able to pronounce it. They always said it perfectly (Hut-tee-sing). It must be their well-trained musical ears!

Thursday, October 30, 1997—
Chicago, B96

It was a beautiful day, so I woke up early and went for a four-hour walk! One of the luxuries of my job was that I often had enough time to see the cities that we visited. Isaac, Taylor, and Zac had school most mornings, so that was a prime time to see the sights. After my extensive self-guided walking tour, I returned to the hotel and met the rest of the gang in the lobby.

We traveled in two separate vans. The Hansons and our managers rode in one, and the rest of us traveled in the other. Peter, our keyboardist/musical director, finally delivered the news that I had anticipated. He was leaving Hanson. I knew his growing frustration with the band would lead to this.

We arrived at the arena and found everything running behind. Our sound check was short because En Vogue, who were also performing, had apparently exceeded their time allotment. After an unsuccessful attempt to get our sound together, we returned to the van and went out for dinner. We stopped at two restaurants before agreeing on a suitable place to eat.

We ended up at a Sheraton hotel near the Rosemont Horizon, the arena where we were performing. We had a great meal before returning to take the stage.

Zac had dressed up for Halloween. I wasn't exactly sure what he was, but he had put on a jumpsuit, moon boots, and something that resembled a motorcycle helmet. It couldn't have been easy playing the drums in that getup! I think his outfit tied in with "Man from Milwaukee," but I could be wrong.

We were excited to play our first concert in an indoor arena. Unfortunately, it turned out to be our worst concert ever. Before we even began, Ike ran over to me on stage and said, "I can't find a guitar pick! Do you have one?" I always keep several in my pocket so I was able to provide him with one. Tay's keyboard had intermittent power throughout the show, our monitor speakers sounded awful, and everyone was distracted and screwed up the parts. These things can happen without a proper

The first restaurant, which we bypassed because we questioned its cleanliness, inspired Walker to share a funny story. He had been a cook in a restaurant when he was fourteen and one time he dropped a stack of hamburgers into a mop bucket. He was so afraid that he might lose his job that he picked them up and threw them on the grill. Gross!

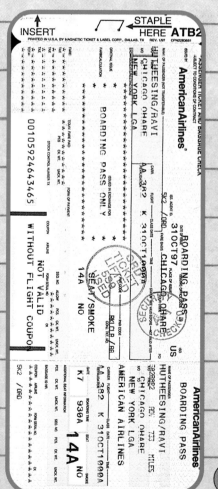

sound check. Our new sound engineer was so horrified that he swore he would never work with us again. Ike was very angry and felt that we had totally embarrassed ourselves. It was a terrible show relative to most and hopefully the lowest point in our adventure together, but the crowd seemed to enjoy it anyway. They can't all be winners!

Saturday, November 8, 1997—
Los Angeles, Rehearsal

I arrived in L.A. late yesterday evening. Scott and I flew from New York together, and we met our new sound engineer, JB, at the airport. He seemed like a cool guy, but it was annoying to have to adjust to new technicians almost every month. (The good part about it was that they were all nice people and I made many more friends with this high turnover!)

Scott and I went to rehearsal around noon. We met Paul Mirkovich, who was Peter's replacement. He's a great guy and we had a lot of fun working together. We jammed for a few hours and then the three of us had lunch.

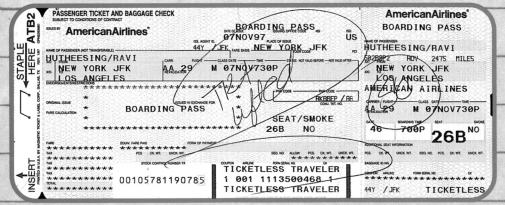

When we returned from our break, we continued to work until the Hanson family arrived at 4:30 P.M. All of us jammed until 9. It was interesting to see the brothers work with a new musician onstage. They were so used to Peter directing them that they were left looking for guidance. However, Hanson had hired Paul as a keyboardist rather than a musical director, so he let them run the band. Fortunately, the change made the band more interactive than it had been. We all offered opinions and suggestions, and instead of one person ruling, we made decisions as a group.

Diana took this opportunity to try to mold Paul into the role she felt he should play. She wanted to make Taylor's keyboard parts more prominent. She offered suggestions to Paul on ways to reshape his sound, trying to prevent him from overshadowing Tay. Her sons occasionally asked her to be quiet and let Paul do his thing. Paul, being the laid-back, friendly guy that he is, did as she asked.

We began rehearsing Christmas songs from the Snowed In CD. "Merry Christmas Baby," "Run Rudolph Run," and "Everybody Loves the Claus" were the ones we focused on. They were fun to play!

After a few hours of work, we ordered in a Chinese dinner and sat around a table in the studio lobby. After an hour, we returned to the stage but didn't rehearse. In fact, Ike and Zac fell asleep on the couch! Tay jammed on his keyboards while his brothers drifted into a deep slumber. Walker eventually woke them up and we all returned to the hotel. The next day, I flew back to New York following an afternoon rehearsal.

Friday, November 14, 1997—
Miami, Rehearsal, Going to see U2

I had a very early flight this morning from New York to Miami. It's a sure sign that one travels too much if the porter recognizes you, and that is exactly what happened. We arrived in Miami, checked into our hotel, and immediately left for the rehearsal studio.

Again, we were working with new technicians but rehearsal was relatively productive. After jamming for a few hours, the guys, Walker, Patricia, Paul, Scott, and I dined out at Boston Market and went to see

U2 in concert. U2 had left VIP passes for us at the entrance, but arrange-ments were sketchy and we couldn't locate them easily.

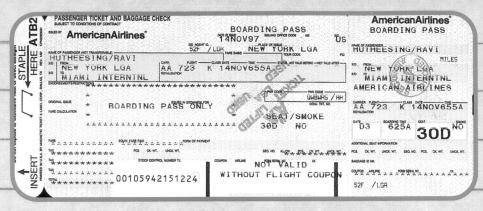

When we arrived at the stadium, no one had arranged for us to park and we sat in traffic for almost an hour. I found the Hansons' frustration with the traffic amusing. They couldn't believe that there were so many people waiting to park. I explained to them, "It's always like this at a concert. This is what your fans go through every time they come to see us!" They had no idea. I guess they had never been to a rock concert as fans.

When we finally entered the stadium grounds and made it up to the ticket booth, we learned the tickets weren't there and we had to walk around to the other side of the stadium. U2 fans recognized the Hansons and created quite a scene. Everyone stared and pointed at us. As usual, the Hansons handled the fans very well in their polite manner.

We finally made it into the stadium moments after the concert had begun. U2 is notorious for starting on time, something Hanson had rarely done! We stood in front of the mixing console where we had a good view. Zac climbed up on a railing behind us to try to see over everyone's heads. U2's sound engineer solved Zac's problem by inviting the three of them to stand behind the console, which was elevated above the audience. After an hour, we went back to our hotel. Zac fell asleep next to me on the floor of the van while the rest of us talked about the concert.

Saturday, November 15, 1997—
Miami, Rehearsal, Australian video shoot

Rehearsal began at 11 A.M. today, although we didn't spend much time practicing. An Australian camera crew took over our studio to film us playing "Run Rudolph Run."

When it was time to perform, we only pretended to play the song. For sound reasons, they used prerecorded music from a tape, but the guys sang their vocals live. We air-strummed our instruments during the song, recording six takes. Despite the fact that we never played a note, the experience was useful in working on our stage presence.

After the camera crew cleared out, we all sat down to a terrific spare-rib lunch and then rehearsed for the rest of the afternoon. KC of KC and the Sunshine Band came by our studio to say hello. He, his daughter, and his wife spent a lot of time chatting with Walker and me. We discussed his long career as well as the instant success that Hanson was experiencing. They seemed like very nice people.

Later in the evening, Taylor, Walker, and I hung out in the parking lot and talked. Tay asked me many questions about my teaching career and my various students. During our conversation, he repeatedly threw a plastic bottle of Coke into the air as high as he could and tried to catch it. Half the time he missed it and the bottle crashed, almost exploding. Walker chose to do the same thing with his soda bottle although he dropped his less frequently. Anticipating a carbonated explosion in the near future, I suggested we return to the studio. We worked for another thirty minutes and then returned to our hotel.

Sunday, November 16, 1997—
Miami, Wing Ding

Today we performed at the Wing Ding in Hollywood, Florida. This was an outdoor concert featuring Hanson and other artists, including

Duncan Sheik and KC and the Sunshine Band.

I left my hotel with Scott and Paul at 9:30 A.M. As is often the case, the stage wasn't ready when we arrived. We hung around under the hot sun until the Hansons arrived to play "Run Rudolph Run" to test the sound. It seemed like an odd selection for such a warm day.

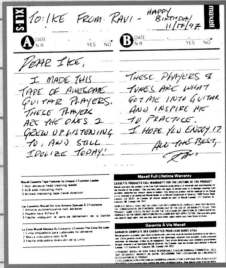

We had a great dressing room (trailer) and the chef, who was one of the best in the area, made cooked-to-order selections and personally delivered them to us. I often took for granted how well we were treated.

We also had plenty of soda, which was cooling in large tubs of ice. Taylor rolled up his sleeves and stuck his arm into the tub searching for a diet soda. After a few seconds, his arm went numb. Zac did the same thing, determined to outlast his brother. All of a sudden, everyone followed suit and we turned our arm dunking into a contest to see who could remain submerged the longest. Stirling, some executives from Mercury, and I took part in the game. I don't think we ever established a winner.

Zac was in rare form today. In the middle of our show, I felt a stream of water hitting my right arm. I looked toward the drums and saw him cracking up with an empty water bottle in his hand. He caught me completely offguard. I couldn't let that go unnoticed and I had no choice but to retaliate. I grabbed my water bottle and Zac looked at me saying, "Go ahead, I dare you!" He didn't have to twist my arm. I got him back! We had a good laugh together, right there onstage. It was definitely a memorable moment.

Zac did something else unusual. Without warning, he broke into a drum solo between songs. The rest of us were all staring at him trying to figure out what was going through his mind. Tay looked at me and shrugged his shoulders, as if to say, "Oh well, whatever." It's hard to reprimand someone on stage in front of more than twenty thousand people! Besides, it actually turned out to be a nice improvisation and made the show unique. When Zac finally finished his display, we got on with the set.

Ike was not pleased with our performance. He felt we bombed, and that the band sounded uninspired. I disagreed, and everyone else seemed to feel good about our show as well.

Following the performance the guys did a "meet and greet," which is a more extensive and intimate "grip and grin" for selected fans only. I went out to mingle with the fans who couldn't get in for autographs and I gave out many guitar picks in addition to signing shirts, hands, album covers . . . whatever it was, I signed it! Soon we climbed aboard our van and returned to the hotel, where I gave Ike a cassette for his birthday. I had compiled recordings of some of my favorite guitar players. Zac got one on his birthday too, except it was a collection of drummers.

Tuesday, November 18, 1997—
New York to Kansas City

A limousine collected Scott and me from the airport to take us to the venue where thousands had already gathered to see our 6 P.M. show. It was still only around two-thirty in the afternoon. The guys showed up for the sound check, and after we did our test, they quickly left for the local radio station to do an on-air promotion for the show.

The day was beautiful—cold air, but a warm sun. Everything got much cooler once the sun set. I was frustrated because there were no dressing rooms to warm up in and my hands were starting to go numb. Eventually, someone brought kerosene heaters to the stage and we all huddled around those.

More importantly, there wasn't much of a technical crew. I had to test Ike's rig and tune his guitars. That wasn't my job! I also set up the percussion for Zac and found water for the band. That wasn't my job either, but no one else was going to do it, and these details were important.

When we did our show it was hard to play because my hands were so cold from being outside all day. Again, Ike had misplaced his guitar pick and had to take one from me. Tay spontaneously decided to stray from our usual set and we threw in an unexpected song, "Run Rudolph Run." He had also started to develop a funny habit of balancing his water bottle on the top of his keyboard. Most of the time it fell off

and rolled toward me, spilling water all over the stage. The funny part was that I usually trapped it, handed it back to him before we started the next song, and he would place it back on top of his keyboard! Then we would do the routine all over again. After the first few shows where this happened, he started realizing it and we would glance at each

other and laugh when-
ever he inadvertently
did it. It became an
ongoing joke between us,
as did the need for me
to always remind him to
transpose his keyboard.
He kept me pretty busy
on our side of the stage!

After the show, we
quickly packed our gear
and the Hansons took a
van to their chartered

plane at a nearby airfield. It was physically hard to say good-bye because fans were approaching us from all angles. As their van pulled away Taylor rolled down his window and yelled, "Ravi, see you later!" Walker reached the backseat and gave me a high-five. Scott and I jumped in our limousine and raced to catch the last flight out of

Kansas City. As we left the vicinity, fans were pounding on the sides of the car and rocking it back and forth. Despite the difficulty in leaving, we made it to the airport with seconds to spare.

Saturday, November 22, 1998—
Atlanta

Despite arriving in Atlanta late last night, we had an early start this morning. I only slept for about four hours, which is a shame when you have a beautiful room in a Ritz Carlton hotel.

I arrived at the venue by 10 A.M. and already fans had started lining up outside the Celebrity Cafe, the bar/restaurant where we were performing. The stage was tiny, much like the ones in the clubs that I used to play. Hanson, as a major act, had never performed in such an atmosphere. However, we were playing an intimate show for four hundred radio contest winners.

After a sound check, we had lunch and I went out to mingle with the fans in line. I met a lot of cool people, signed a bunch of autographs, and took pictures with some groupies. When we started at 4 P.M., the fans were ready. It was a lot of fun playing in such close quarters, with the crowd right on top of us, screaming and crying in amazement. We all took the stage together, although the guys began with the usual acoustic set, playing by themselves. However, when Zac came on stage, he couldn't find any of the hand-percussion instruments. The crew had

not placed them where they were expected to be. Walker jumped on stage with a look of urgency and searched for the bag. I hadn't realized what was happening so I asked Zac if everything was all right. He looked up at me and in a frustrated tone said, "No, everything is not all right!" Walker asked if anyone knew where the percussion bag was. I took a quick glance around and spotted it behind the bass amplifier. I jumped over Scott, grabbed the bag, and Walker, Zac, and I all put our hands inside to pull out the shakers and tambourine. Despite the difficult beginning, the remainder of the acoustic performance was smooth.

We had one major foul-up during the electric set, perhaps the single biggest screwup of any show. Taylor started "I Will Come to You" in the wrong key. He had completed the entire piano introduction before realizing his mistake, and he had no choice but to stop and begin again. It could have been a very embarrassing moment, but instead it was a highlight of the show. Tay handled it very professionally, making a joke out of it.

While the Hansons conducted a lengthy "meet and greet," I hung out with the fans in the parking lot, signing a ton of autographs and posing for pictures.

> **T**here was a very attractive blond girl standing right in front of Taylor and me. I had actually met her outside earlier. She told me to tell Taylor that he was supposed to marry her. Before we took the stage, I relayed the message, and asked him after the show if he noticed the girl. He said, "Yeah, she's really cute!" I told him that she was the one I had mentioned before, but he was shy and didn't pursue the lead.

A reporter came up to me and asked a question that caught me off guard. "What do you think about the Michael Hutchence (lead singer for INXS) incident?" I'd no idea that he had hanged himself the day before. We had been so busy that the news escaped us. What was particularly eerie was that I just saw him a couple of months earlier when we taped the Weird Al Show and INXS was on Jay Leno.

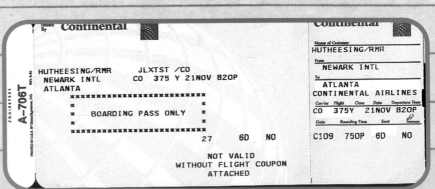

After the Hansons had finished their "meet and greet," we boarded the tour bus and drove to the airplane. A line of cars followed us to the small private airfield where the Hansons' charter awaited. (They had been city hopping so they reserved a private plane for several days). The bus then took the rest of us to the main airport and we departed for home.

In New York, a limousine met me at the airport. Thirty minutes into the ride, I realized that I had left my journal on the plane, which upset me because I had been documenting my entire Hanson experience.* I decided to make all further entries directly into my laptop computer.

*About one week later, an employee of the airline phoned me to say that he found my journal in a seat pocket. I had written my telephone number on the journal only two days before I had lost it. The gentleman mailed it to me a couple of weeks later —thank you, sir!

7
Christmas Crunch

December was quite a month! Every aspect of Hanson was booming: the schedules were busier, the concerts were more prestigious, and band politics were at an all-time high. We performed in arguably the most famous arena in the world, for the president of the United States, and on one of the most-watched live programs on TV. We also performed shows with other noteworthy artists including the Wallflowers, Backstreet Boys, Celine Dion, Fiona Apple, Sarah McLachlan, and Aerosmith.

Diana and the young Hansons joined us for most of the month. The holidays created a festive atmosphere and we focused on songs from *Snowed In*. We were all in the spirit of the holidays!

Sunday, December 7, 1997—
New York, Rehearsal

I decided to take the train to New York for my 11 A.M. rehearsal. I should have anticipated the large crowds of travelers since it was a Sunday close to Christmas. The first train was so crowded that I decided to wait for the next, knowing that this would make me at least twenty minutes late to rehearsal. Unfortunately, the Hansons were teaching me that tardiness made no difference. They were always late and rarely acknowledged it.

I arrived at 11:30 A.M. and still sat around waiting. The Hansons showed up at noon. Jason, the bodyguard, was not with them, which was unusual. We rehearsed for about three hours and then had a big Chinese meal. After lunch, Shania Twain and Mutt Lang (a legendary producer) dropped by to say hello. Ike, Tay, Zac, Diana, and I hung out and talked with them for a bit. Zac was acting goofy around them. Knowing him, I realized that he was being his playful self. However, others often misinterpreted his actions and found him obnoxious. After Shania and Mutt left, Diana asked Zac why he was acting that way. He said he didn't know. She then asked him if he would have acted differently if Mutt were interested in producing their next album. Zac shrugged his shoulders, said, "no," and started running around the studio.

The guys were supposed to leave for Las Vegas to be presenters at the Billboard Music Awards. Because of our hectic schedule, coupled with the brothers' colds, they canceled their travel plans. We were all concerned that Ike, Tay, and Zac were going to be sick for our most important shows. Patricia (tour manager) supplied them with constant doses of the herbal remedies Echinacea-Golden Seal. They were disgusted by the stuff but consumed it anyway. Speaking of disgusting stuff, Tay offered me a mint. He bought a box of them in London and assured me that they were really good. I accepted and placed it in my mouth. Moments later, I realized it was sort of like a very potent cough drop and my sinuses were burning from the pungent flavor. Tay likes to play tricks like that and thoroughly enjoyed my reaction!

Since they had called off their trip, they decided to rehearse again the next day, which was originally a day off. I had to bite my tongue because I wanted to say something about how I hated the way they changed the schedule and assumed that everyone would "dance along." The reality was that I didn't have much planned that I couldn't change, and I could use the extra money.

Tuesday, December 9, 1997—
New York, Jingle Ball, Madison Square Garden

I took the train and a taxi to Madison Square Garden, arriving around 10 A.M. Immediately I ran into Stan, our lighting director, who led me to the dressing room. I was the first band member to arrive so I went onstage and tested my

gear. The Hansons and other band members arrived soon after I finished. After doing a sound check they returned to their hotel for a press conference. I stayed at the arena most of the day, watching the other bands sound check and absorbing the experience of MSG. I had seen many of my guitar and rock 'n' roll heroes here, and now I was going to take the legendary stage. I wasn't sure that the Hansons could truly appreciate this. They hadn't struggled as musicians or climbed the "musical ladder."

I was unusually nervous all day and went out around 5 P.M. to have a slice of pizza with a friend. Hanson fans stopped me for pictures and autographs, and two girls actually kissed me while someone else took a picture. When I returned to the arena, a girl recognized me and started to freak out. I gave her a guitar pick and a handshake, and went to the dressing room. My old guitar teacher and his daughter arrived—I had arranged pass-

JOHN "RATSO" GERARDI

es for them. As I was greeting them, the Hansons drove up in their van and I introduced them all.

Again, Jason was not with them. Instead, there was a new bodyguard, Darrell. He seemed like a cool guy, but I wondered why they had made the change. I decided to add that to the list of things I may never know. I have been told that the rule of thumb is to "never ask what you don't absolutely need to know."

Steven Tyler of Aerosmith came to our dressing room with his wife and daughters, including Liv, to say hello. It was so cool to meet Steven in person, especially since I grew up listening to Aerosmith. Among the other celebrities present were Marla Maples, Lisa Marie Presley, and all the other bands scheduled to perform.

When it was time to hit the stage, we slapped high-fives and rocked! The show was full of energy and very smooth. The vibe pumped me up so much that I moved out farther into the middle of the stage than usual during Ike's and my guitar break in "Where's the Love." We all agreed that it was one of our best shows to date, and the eighteen thousand fans were ecstatic.

I invited my friends to our dressing room after the show to meet the Hansons. As a courtesy, I asked Walker if it would be all right. He said yes, but was clearly reluctant. Only a few minutes after they entered, he said, "Your friends need to leave now." That annoyed me because it was <u>our</u> dressing room and these were my <u>friends</u>. He'd never been that rude to me before. As I escorted my friends out, Stirling and Christopher asked to speak with me. I thought to myself, "Oh great, what have I done now?" To my surprise, they asked if everything regarding my friends was all right. I said everything was fine, but I did share my disappointment in Walker with them. Both Stirling and Christopher apologized because they recognized that I was upset about it. It was very kind of them to inquire.

While hanging around backstage, I ran into the Wallflowers. The drummer, Mario, congratulated me on the show. Jakob Dylan was standing there so I put an arm around him and said, "You must be Jason." Oops! Mario quickly corrected me. (I don't know why I said that. I knew what his name was!)

After that embarrassment, I hung out with the Hansons, and we all watched Aerosmith, who put on a great show. Ike, Tay, Zac, and I stood on the side of the stage. I kept trying to reposition Zac so he could see the drummer. The guy played some cool stuff, but Zac seemed more interested in Steven Tyler. The fans behind us screamed for Hanson, and as always, the guys gave them what they wanted and waved.

The Hansons left to go back to their hotel, but I stayed by myself to watch the Wallflowers. They sounded great. As soon as they finished, I hailed a taxi and returned to my hotel. We all skipped the after party.

Wednesday, December 10, 1997—

Boston, Kissmas

At 6:45 A.M., Scott and I took a taxi to the hotel where the crew was staying. There, we boarded a coach and headed for Boston to play two separate shows in one day. The main show was at Avalon, where we performed with the Wallflowers, Michael Bolton, Fiona Apple, and several others. We arrived there at 11:30 A.M. Paul, Scott, and I sat around for hours while the crew set up. The Hansons were supposed to arrive by 1 P.M., but they got lost and didn't show up until 3:30 P.M. By that time, we had scrapped the Avalon sound check and moved to the second venue, a club called Mama Kin.

We did a sound check once the Hansons arrived and then retreated to our dressing room above the stage. At show time we headed down the fire escape to enter the

I became the Hansons' source of information for getting to the right place. We were in constant communication by cell phone. While mingling with the fans, posing for pictures, signing autographs, and giving out guitar picks, I was directing the Hansons to the venue by phone. "Okay, do you see Fenway Park? Is it on your right? Okay, turn right at the end of the bleachers. Keep going. **Do you see me standing in the road, waving my arms?**" That's basically how it went.

stage through the back door. Six hundred screaming fans had packed the room. It was a reasonably good show, although the Hansons felt that it was a poor performance. They followed it with a "grip and grin" and then we all relaxed in the tour bus, watching the movie Dirty Rotten Scoundrels. After we got the cue to take the stage at Avalon, we played for an audience that was definitely not our crowd. They were receptive, but not responsive. The Hansons felt that it was a terrible show and they were totally bummed out. We got off to a bad start because the radio jock who introduced us was not particularly inspired, or at least Ike didn't feel that he was. After the introduction, Ike proceeded to tell the crowd not to listen to the emcee, but to get ready to rock because "this is a Hanson show!" I couldn't figure out what he was doing. I knew he meant no harm, but I don't think he used his best judgment on this one. Teasing a radio jock does not help to get your songs on the air!

I chatted with Michael Bolton and Meredith Brooks upstairs in the dressing room while I was waiting to leave. We returned to New York in the same buses that brought us to Boston.

Rumor had it that someone in the other bus had a little incident in the bathroom and stank up the whole cabin! Someone in our bus renamed the tour the "MMMPlop" tour.

Friday, December 12, 1997—
New York—Washington—New York,
"Christmas in Washington" dress rehearsal

I woke up this morning with a terrible cold and sore throat. However, I had no choice but to get through a very hectic day. A limousine collected me at 11:30 A.M. to take me to Newark Airport.

I arrived in plenty of time and grabbed a burger and fries with our publicist and an executive from Mercury. After the quick meal, we went to the gate. Soon Hanson and most of the entourage, including Patricia and Paul, arrived. I didn't know that both of the Chavarrias were coming on this trip but I assumed it was because we were performing for the president of the United States.

We arrived at Ronald Reagan Washington National Airport and traveled by van to the National Building Museum, where the concert was to take place. There was a long debate because the producers of the show did not want the entire band onstage for the performance. They said there was no room for anyone other than the three Hansons. Paul requested a trial run to prove that we could do it. We started to set it up and it was obvious that it would work, but the producers stopped us midway and said no. The Hansons continued to argue, but they eventually lost. Scott and I were going to be in the orchestra pit and Paul (keyboardist) was going to be behind the stage and completely out of sight. This was very insulting to the three of us, but particularly to Paul, who deserved to be visibly included in the event. I could tell that Ike, Tay, and Zac were genuinely unhappy about it, but I don't think anyone outside of the band particularly cared.

After setting up as directed, a large choir walked on stage surrounding the guys. I suppose the Hansons knew that a choir was singing backup on "Merry Christmas Baby," but I had no idea. I couldn't believe that these forty or so people were on stage, while Paul, Scott, and I were offstage because of space constraints!

The rehearsal was okay, but we missed our evening flight back to New York because of all the debating. We raced to the airport and literally ran through the building to make the next one. Everyone, including the Hanson family, carried instruments and cases, and Taylor was holding a large gingerbread house that we were given. We arrived at the gate only to find that the airline had canceled our flight. Our last chance out of there was the next flight, an hour later. We all hung out in the lounge area and griped about the horrible circumstances of the day, then boarded the single-class, general seating (no seat assignments) plane. Taylor was sitting in an empty row, and when no one sat with him, he hopped into the seat next to me. He grabbed the in-flight magazine and immediately opened it to a picture of a beautiful girl in a bikini. We shared it with the entourage surrounding us, and then periodically referred to it during the flight. We had fun chatting about nothing in particular. When we arrived at La Guardia, we all split up.

Saturday, December 13, 1997—
New York, Saturday Night Live

A stretch limo collected me from home at 3:30 P.M. and when I arrived at the NBC building, fans were waiting on the streets. As I got out of the car, people started yelling my name and taking my picture. It was fun getting all this attention! I went up to the dressing room and everyone, including Darrell, who was standing guard at the door, was there. I'm usually the first to arrive!

Everyone was talking about the headaches in Washington. If I overheard correctly, the producer of the presidential event called our manager and suggested that we not show up for the actual show the next day. I wondered if that was some type of warning or threat.

Another debate started, as if yesterday's hadn't been frustrating enough. The SNL producers and Hanson disagreed on the songs for that night's show. Originally, the Hansons did not want to do "MMMBop" because they felt that the audience was ready for something new from them. However, SNL wanted us to play the "summer anthem" and we eventually agreed. Still, the guys wanted to play "Merry Christmas Baby" first, but the SNL producers were set on "MMMBop" as the opener. Taylor insisted that the viewing

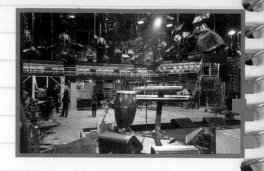

audience was going to think that we couldn't play anything else. "People are going to label us that 'MMMBop' band," he'd say. After much negotiation, we agreed to perform "MMMBop" first, and SNL agreed to put us on

during the opening half hour, when it had its largest viewing audience. It is extremely rare to have the band on before the SNL news segment, so Hanson management was pleased with the decision. I sometimes wonder if these arguments were more about egos than actual issues.

We sat around for a while, did a sound check, and had a nice dinner in the studio dining room. I sat at a table with Isaac, Taylor, and Zac. Ike broke some bad news to me. He had left the birthday present that I had given him in Miami—the mix tape that I made.

Zac told me that there was a weird picture of me in the dressing room. I asked what it was and he said, "There's, like, two girls kissing you, and one is wearing a Santa hat." I immediately knew what picture it was—the one with the two girls who kissed me outside Madison Square Garden days earlier. How did that get here? After dinner I went to the dressing room and Diana said, "I think this one is for you" and she handed me the picture. Apparently, the girls had asked an NBC security guard to give it to the Hansons. On the back of the picture it said, "We love Ravi," which was how Diana knew it was for me.

At 8 P.M., we did a live dress rehearsal in front of an audience. The actual live show began at 11:30 P.M., so we returned to the dressing room to rest for a bit. But instead there was lots of activity—the people who ran the official Hanson Web site, Hansonline, were trying to upload digital images from the dress rehearsal, but I'm not sure that they ever got them to work properly. I believe they were trying to use Walker's digital camera to cybercast the event, including backstage scenes.

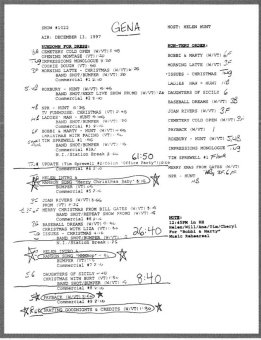

Soon enough it was time for the real show to begin. As agreed, we played "MMMBop" first and it sounded good. We returned to the dressing rooms for approximately thirty minutes until it was time for the guys to perform a skit with Helen Hunt, while the rest of us stood in the wings and watched. The guys did well. The premise of the sketch was that Helen and another cast member took the Hansons hostage in an elevator and tortured them by forcing them to listen to "MMMBop." Ike and Zac succumbed to the torture, but Tay managed to survive it. Straight after the Hansons' acting debut, we performed a practically flawless version of "Merry Christmas Baby," which sounded great with the <u>SNL</u> horn section playing with us. Zac finished the song by yelling into his microphone "Merry Christmas everybody! I feel so alone!" Tay just smiled at the camera, not knowing how to react.

After the show was the annual <u>SNL</u> Christmas Party. The Hansons were tired and elected to return to their hotel. However, almost everyone else from the production went, including our managers, some executives from Mercury, Paul, and I, as well as Helen Hunt and Jack Nicholson (our hosts on <u>SNL</u>). I saw several other famous people, too, including Dan Aykroyd. We had a great time and didn't get back to the hotel until 4:15 A.M. My wake-up call the next day was at 6:30 A.M.—Ugh!

Sunday, December 14, 1997—
Washington, D.C., President Clinton

Today we taped "Christmas in Washington" in front of the president of the United States of America. It was also one of the few times when our entire entourage traveled on the same plane.

We arrived at the airport an hour early for our 9:30 A.M. flight. Stirling bought everyone a cinnamon raisin bun and a carton of milk. I'm not much of a milk drinker, but the Hanson family contributed greatly to the milk industry. I imagine that's why they agreed to do the famous milk mustache ad. I learned of another thing that Tay and I had in common—we both hate raisins.

Patricia checked everyone in at the gate; however, the airline clerk was extremely slow, and when we proceeded to the plane, we saw that the jetway had already pulled away from the aircraft. One shouldn't be late for the president of the United States! An argument broke out between our people and the airline employees. The plane was still at the gate and if the airline had wanted, they could have boarded us. After all, they were the ones who delayed us. The plane eventually disappeared down the runway.

We moved to the presidential lounge (how appropriate) to wait for the next flight to Washington. Chances were we were going to miss the dress rehearsal so the authorities at the airline called the White House to explain the situation. We wanted to be sure that everyone in Washington knew that this was not Hanson's fault. After reissuing our tickets, we boarded the next flight out of New Jersey. The airline tried to accommodate us by allowing the plane to leave a few minutes early.

After a shaky liftoff, we were finally headed for Washington. About fifteen minutes into the flight, the plane started to bank heavily to the right. It appeared that the pilot was turning back. I remarked to our sound engineers, who were sitting directly in front of me, that something seemed odd. One of them rang his call button. Apparently, he saw the Fasten Seat Belt sign flicker and assumed that there was something wrong with the power system. While inquiring, the pilot summoned the flight attendant to the cockpit. As she returned, the pilot announced that two of three power generators had failed and we had to make an emergency landing back at Newark.

Many passengers were frightened because the plane fishtailed all the way to the airport and a burning smell drifted into the cabin. As we touched down, I looked out the window and saw fire engines and emergency vehicles chasing our plane. We landed safely and deplaned ahead of the other passengers. The airline delayed another flight so that we could try to get airborne quickly.

Everyone was getting nervous at this point. Amy, our stylist, even suggested that perhaps this was some type of omen. This presidential gig had certainly been difficult from the start. A few members of our entourage were not comfortable enough to try again, but the rest of us boarded the next flight.

As we walked to the gate, Paul (keyboardist) remarked that all the airports were beginning to look the same. I asked him what he meant and he said, "This airport looks just like Newark." I replied, "This is Newark." Paul had been asleep throughout the entire incident and assumed that we had landed in Washington.

A former secret agent collected us at National Airport and drove us to the National Building Museum. Security officials thoroughly hand-searched each of our bags and then we walked through a metal detector. Isaac, Taylor, and Zac received All Access passes and the rest of us wore small red buttons that said 1997. The officials told us to wear the buttons high so they could easily be seen. Apparently, secu-

rity wouldn't look twice before taking action.

We immediately set up on stage and rehearsed "Merry Christmas Baby." The conservative producers of this event were unhappy about having a "pop" band in the first place, and our tardiness only furthered their concerns. However, many members of Congress requested extra tickets when they found out that we were performing. Everyone wanted to bring the kids! Following our rehearsal, we sat around for hours with little to do. We ate dinner, put on our performance clothes, and hung out.

The guys wore slick outfits: Ike was sporting a satin suit and Taylor was dressed in velvet. The rest of us were dressed in nice black pants and shirts, provided by a Hanson-endorsed designer.

The Hanson family went to meet the President in the main reception area. I tried to tag along, but security stopped me approximately thirty feet away, so I decided to watch from there. Several Secret Service agents approached me and asked if I could get the Hansons to autograph pictures for their children, which I managed to do. I wasn't going to mess with the Secret Service!

Taylor saw me standing there and waved. The Hansons stood in line and one after another shook President Clinton's hand and then greeted the First Lady, Hillary, and their daughter,

Chelsea. While they all stood in a circle for thirty seconds exchanging pleasantries, Tay glanced toward me and pointed, and then the President gestured in my direction. I hesitate to say that he waved to me, but it seemed like an acknowledgment.

We performed well but Ike's amplifier didn't work and one couldn't hear his guitar. Following the show, he came up to me and said, "Thanks for saving me!" However, because I was off to the side in the orchestra pit, I had no idea he was having problems. Despite the glitch, President Clinton seemed to enjoy our performance. He smiled throughout the song, subtly "bopping" his head to the rhythm. The First Lady and Chelsea were more reserved and simply watched the band with "presidential" smiles. After leaving the stage, the Hansons went to the dressing room to do some interviews and the rest of us watched the remainder of the show. Following the event, Christopher and I attended a cocktail reception, while everyone else hung out in the dressing room.

Thursday, December 18, 1997—

New York, *David Letterman*

I arrived at the legendary Ed Sullivan Theater at 3 P.M. Knowing that I had already played in this venue seven months earlier was quite comforting.

Many fans greeted me near the backstage door, including the two girls who had kissed me ten days earlier outside Madison Square Garden.

Once inside, Christopher came up to me and asked if I had heard the news about actor and comedian Chris Farley. I hadn't, so he informed me that he had died that morning. He decided not to tell the Hansons until after our show. They were big fans of Farley. The eerie thing was that when we played Saturday Night Live, I asked the talent coordinator if Farley was going to be attending the Christmas party that evening. His response was "Maybe, if he isn't dead yet." I chose not to pursue the conversation at that time, but I realized that the people who knew him sensed he was close to the end.

We did a quick sound check and camera block (testing of camera angles) and then returned to our dressing rooms. I went outside for a

breath of fresh air and the fans began to chant "Ravi, Ravi, Ravi."
That had never happened before! I went back into the theater and
stood in the wings. Ike, Tay, Zac, and the other band members joined me,
with Ike sporting a leather jacket and Tay decked out in leather pants.

We all took the stage following Leslie Nielsen's interview and played a
kicking version of "Run Rudolph Run." The CBS Orchestra's horn section
joined us for the tune. After the show, we quickly went to Dave's office
and the Hansons' photographer took a picture of the guys with the host.
Paul (keyboardist) and I left the building to go back to our hotel. Many
fans were outside waiting for the Hansons to leave. We signed autographs and I gave away handfuls of guitar picks. Then we jumped into
a taxi and went to the hotel.

Friday, December 19, 1997—
New York, Marathon End-Of-Year Day

My wake-up call came at 4:30 A.M. and a limousine collected Paul,
Scott, and me thirty minutes later. We went to the ABC studios to perform on Good Morning America. Following the sound check, we hung out
for almost two hours, chatting and watching cartoons in our dressing
room. Stirling went out and bought egg sandwiches for everyone. The
guys did an interview before we performed. Ike got into this story
about the oil industry in Tulsa. He was attempting to cover up Zac's
suggestion that almost everyone in Oklahoma is a hick. He obviously did-
n't mean that, but Ike tried to come to his rescue and rambled on
about stuff that he didn't really know. During a commercial I jokingly
said to him, "When this is over, I'd love to talk more with you about the
oil industry in Tulsa." He laughed and said, "Well, I don't know, I was trying to cover for Zac." It was all pretty funny and that is part of what
makes these guys so charming.

We performed "Merry Christmas Baby," "Run Rudolph Run," and "I Will
Come to You." It was fine although our managers were fuming because
the cameras panned on some young kids in the audience, and Hanson
was trying to abolish the notion that all Hanson fans were young kids. A
ferocious yelling match broke out between our management and the

ABC producers. I found it hard to believe that it was worth threatening our relationship with a major broadcasting company over something that was water under the bridge. It was a live TV show and it was over! Following the fireworks, we returned to our hotel around 10 A.M.

Our driver collected us at noon and brought us to CNN, where we did a spot on <u>Show Biz Today</u>. It was relatively painless, as we performed "Merry Christmas Baby" and "Run Rudolph Run" in a small studio without a live audience. The guys also gave an interview that I think came across badly. Maybe they were getting too comfortable in front of the camera because if one didn't know them personally, one could easily misconstrue their sarcasm. Paul, Scott, and I decided to go down to Little Italy in lower Manhattan for lunch. It was a nice break from what had already been a busy morning. However, the day was far from over.

Our driver collected us from the restaurant and we battled heavy traffic to get to the Meadowlands Convention Center in New Jersey, where we were performing at the "MMMBop Ball" for three to four thousand fans. We were late in arriving and went right to the stage to sound check, followed by the usual two-hour "time kill" in the dressing rooms. It had been such a long day and everyone was restless. Ike and Zac were throwing each other around the room. It was quite funny, but I couldn't imagine what would happen if one of them got hurt. A few young fans came back to say hello. One girl, who couldn't have been more than ten years old, was so starstruck that she literally froze. Zac went up to her, grabbed her shoulders, and shook her, yelling in a goofy voice, "Breathe! Somebody help her!"

Just before we started the show, I paid a visit to the bathroom, which was about fifty feet away from our dressing room door. I saw Darrell standing guard outside the men's room, so I figured one of the guys was in there. I walked in and Tay turned to me and said, "Hey, aren't you that guy Ravi, the famous guitarist?" I said, "Yes, you've heard of me." He responded, "Yeah, of course. You have those three Hanson brothers who back you up, right?" Tay and I often carried on these sarcastic conversations with each other. Earlier in the year we'd

say stuff like that and then
acknowledge that we were
kidding. But after spending so
much time together, we carried on as if it were the truth.
He is fun that way. I think
that much of our friendship
was based on our similar sense

of humor and ability to understand each other without explanations.
We also always talked during TV commercial breaks and sound checks
since we stood next to each other on stage.

   Finally, we went on stage and did the full set. After the show the
Hansons had to catch a flight back to Tulsa. They hadn't been home
in a while and were looking forward to spending the holidays relaxing.
Ike gave each of us a gift—a Swiss Army credit card utility kit. I
wished the Hansons a Merry Christmas and we all hugged good-bye.

1997

ended with our intention of regrouping in February '98, to commence a four- to six-month world tour. Throughout the month of January, Patricia kept me advised on the constant changes in the Hanson schedule. Because of the lack of certainty as to when the tour would begin, I elected to take some short trips to Europe and Los Angeles to promote my solo career. However, Hanson was still my priority and I was prepared to change my schedule at a moment's notice.

Upon my arrival in Los Angeles at the end of January, I received a telephone call from one of Hanson's managers. He informed me that he had had a conversation with Walker and that for reasons he did not understand himself, the Hanson family had decided to replace me with a friend from home.

I was surprised and disappointed, but knew that job security never existed for anyone working with Hanson, given the number of unexplained personnel changes that past year. I also realized that because I had dedicated so much time, heart, and energy to this band, I would feel the void greatly. It was just something that I would have to deal with.

What disappointed me most was that the guys never talked to me about it directly. Nevertheless, I had many wonderful experiences and made some great new friends.

Despite a six-month awkward silence between the Hansons and myself, I trusted that our friendships remained intact. In July 1998, I was in Seattle, at the same time as Hanson. I bought a ticket to their concert, which turned out to be the one that they taped for the Albertane tour video and CD, and with great difficulty managed to get backstage after the show. I was nervous because we hadn't corresponded since they let me go and I had no idea how they felt about me. As I'd hoped, we still seemed to be friends.

Ike came out first and we talked for about ten minutes. We discussed the Hanson tour and plans for a new album. Before he left I gave him a copy of my new CD, and he said he would send his brothers out. About ten minutes later, Tay came out and gave me a big hug. He seemed very excited to see me and we chatted for about a half hour. Tay offered me a mint and I accepted. Moments later I was overwhelmed by menthol. I can't believe I fell for that trick again. He did that to me months ago! It was great seeing him again. Zac also stopped by briefly, but I think he felt a little uncomfortable. Nevertheless, he was affectionate and friendly.

None of us brought up the issues that had come between us. I think we were all just happy to see one another. This was an opportunity to revive friendships rather than bring up sore subjects.

We have stayed in touch since our icebreaker in Seattle. Whether or not we ever work together again, I hope we will remain friends. A single year may not be much during the course of a lifetime, but 1997 was one that I will never forget.

"Hanson" June 26, 1997
Thursday, Summer in the City

5:00 A.M. Crew arrive *Fox After Breakfast*
212 5th Avenue @ 26th Street (Corner)

6:30 A.M. Ravi car service home to Fox 26th & 5th Avenue

7:00 A.M. Hanson van picks up Paul C.

7:30 A.M. Van arrives at Le Parker Meridien
Paul & Jason in lobby on standby

7:30 A.M. Stirling & Amy depart from hotel from 56th Street side in cargo van

7:45 A.M. Hanson departs hotel on the 56th Street side of hotel
This will be your 7 passenger van

8:00 A.M. Arrive *Fox After Breakfast*
212 5th Avenue @ 26th Street

8:15 - 8:45 A.M. Sound check and rehearsal

8:45 A.M. - 9:00 A.M. KDWB phoner Minneapolis radio station Z-100
(3-minute taped interview)

9:00 A.M. *Fox After Breakfast* goes on air

9:00 A.M. - 9:45 A.M. The following things will occur:
(Not necessarily in this order):
Entrance to studio on roller blades
Couch time
Show involvement with hosts
Fox news "mini" interview
Access Hollywood interview

9:40 A.M. Hanson moves to street for performance

9:45 A.M. "MMMBop" (2 1/2-minute version)

9:48 A.M. - 9:55 A.M. "Thinking of You" performed in this time period

9:55 A.M. Show wraps

"Hanson" June 26, 1997
Thursday, Summer in the City

2:30 P.M.	*Entertainment Weekly* photo shoot wraps
2:30 P.M. - 2:45 P.M.	Cool down & chill out period!
2:45 P.M.	Depart Chelsea Piers for Coney Island
3:45 P.M.	Coney Island interview with Jancee Dunn/ *Rolling Stone* article
5:00 P.M.	*Rolling Stone* interview wraps
6:30 P.M.	Arrive Le Parker Meridien
6:45 P.M.	Tentative meeting with Steve Greenberg @ hotel (Approximately 1/2 hour meeting) Finish & go relax!!!!!!!!!!!!!!!!!